D1095626

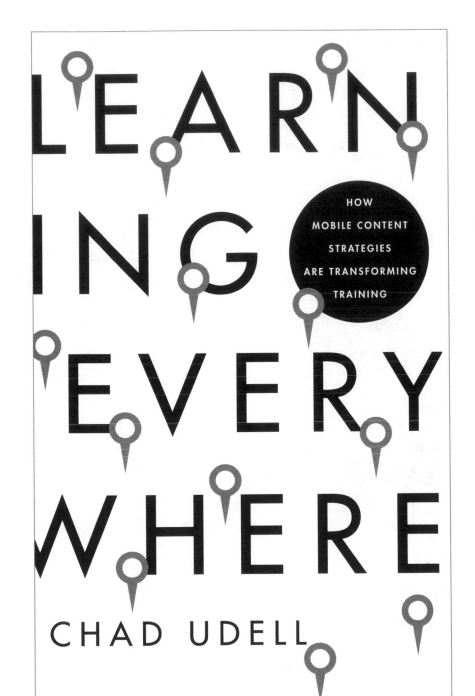

LEARNING

EVERY

WHERE

HOW MOBILE CONTENT STRATEGIES ARE TRANSFORMING TRAINING

CHAD UDELL

DEDICATION

To my loving and supportive wife, Renee, and my beautiful children,
Sophia, Liam and Carter.
Without you, none of this would be possible.
Thank you. I love you all.

rockbench
PUBLISHING

Rockbench Publishing Corp.
6101 Stillmeadow Dr.,
Nashville, TN 37211
www.rockbench.com

1640 King Street Box 1443
Alexandria, VA 22313-1443
www.atsd.org

Author: Chad Udell
Editor: Gary Woodill, Ed.D.
Contributing Editor: Adam Bockler
Illustrator: Matt Forcum

Cover and Interior Design by Faceout Studio

Library of Congress Control Number: 2012939837
Printed in the United States of America
First edition, 2012
ISBN: 978-1-60544-017-0

CONTENTS

FOREWORD

I have often thought that someone should write a comprehensive mobile learning book, but it should be from a practitioner who has vast experiences in this industry. Before "Learning Everywhere," there were authors who wrote about what others had done, or books that targeted specific areas such as instructional design for mobile or programming for mobile, but none that came from an author with both the accolades and scars of creating effective mobile learning solutions. Chad Udell definitely speaks from extensive experience, offers a lot of original thought, and has a talent for writing understandable explanations. His conversational writing style makes one think that Chad is talking directly to them -- a very comprehensive, but easy read. It is obvious that he loves what he does and is good at it.

Whether you are just beginning to investigate mLearning or have a project or two under your belt, this will surely become your "go to" book. From strategy and planning, content choices, taking action and getting started, all the way through design, development and lifecycle, Chad provides examples, abundant questions and checklists and encourages you to "scribble in the sidebar." He uses the mobile first strategy, while always thinking about the experiences of the user to guide his recommendations.

I especially like the categorized approach for different delivery opportunities with his four types of content for mobile delivery. This is a unique framing and will guide your strategic thinking well.

His practical examples, like the eLearning to mLearning example in Chapter 6, offer some real-world grounding to these bigger ideas. He definitely sees the opportunities for creating improved learning experiences with mobile and shares willingly. This is a "how to manual" for mobile learning.

For the past two years I have been curating articles and information on mobile learning for a weekly newsletter, and have been struck by the increasing amounts of materials on mobile learning (some good, some bad). Having retired for the second time, but still very interested in the opportunities for mobile in education and training, I continue with the newsletter. I'm not sure how I could possibly keep up with mobile if I were still working full-time, but will definitely be referring to "Learning Everywhere" going forward. I wish that I had had a book like this to refer organizations to over the past six years of presentations and workshops.

I believe we are only at the beginning of this mobile revolution. Already more people have mobile subscriptions than have access to electricity or safe drinking water (Chetan Sharma Consulting) and the average person has their cellphone within reach 14 hours per day (Impiger Mobile). We are already using these devices for media and entertainment, travel and mapping, banking and finance, and shopping. Why not for learning?

To paraphrase Chad's closing sentence in Chapter 8, the potential of mobile for learning is enormous, and we really haven't seen anything yet. It is up to you, the readers of this book, to make certain that we take advantage of all these exciting opportunities for continuous life-long learning everywhere.

Judy Brown
Mobile Learning Analyst

PREFACE

My strong desire and the intent of this book is to offer you, the reader, immediately applicable strategic thinking about mobile learning. I wanted to create a book to provide real-world, practical guidance that is usable and implementable and valuable.

I kind of "fell" into learning. I started as a graphic designer and an art historian. I got hooked on interactivity and digital, hacking away nights on my now ancient PowerMac 7100 while at university. Soon, I was enamored with not only making things look good, but also "making them work." This inevitably led to learning a lot of programming languages and toolkits as well as some fun nights fueled by caffeine (I worked at a coffee shop back then).

Flash forward to now, and I am sometimes not quite sure how I got here. After getting familiar with Web design, I built a lot of games. Many of these were in the "edu-tainment" vein, created for the preschool and elementary school age groups. Later, as the topics and content got more and more learning focused, I naturally began designing and building eLearning. Eventually, almost everything I was building was educational in nature, whether it was a game, eLearning course or an installation or kiosk at a museum or tradeshow. It's strange how things work out that way, sometimes.

I do know that I love what I am doing, and my fascination has evolved from not only figuring out how to make things work, but also helping people figure out how to use those things and how to learn while doing it. I love helping people learn - of this there is no doubt. This love of helping people learn has continued for me with mobile after the introdution of the iPhone. I dabbled a bit with building content for feature phones via J2ME and Processing, but I really didn't get interested in mobile until multitouch input and touchscreens came along.

In creating this book, a mobile learning book focused on real-world design built around the concept of content strategy, I hope that I will help lay the groundwork for a workplace transformation for you. This is the world we work in; the training we create is only as good as the results it achieves, after all. Properly designed and developed mobile learning that aligns with your overall business strategy via a sound content strategy does just this.

I hope you enjoy this book. I hope it helps you help others learn. If it does, please let me know. I always like hearing success stories. If you read this book, though, and fail horribly, keep it to yourself. ;-)

ACKNOWLEDGEMENTS

This is my first book. It would not have been possible without a long list of colleagues, mentors, friends and advisors. I do hope I don't leave any out here. My apologies in advance if I have.

First and foremost, I wish to thank the staff of Float Mobile Learning and our parent company, The Iona Group. This dedicated team of professionals, which I have been lucky enough to call my friends and coworkers for the last nine years, makes going to work a true pleasure. It's great to have a support network and to be able to depend on these people on a daily basis.

I would like to give a special note of thanks and appreciation to the leaders of Float and Iona, Tom Marchal and John Feser. They encouraged me to write a book, and specifically, one that would be of value to companies and learning organizations of all sizes and shape.

Thanks to Jim Ferolo, our outstanding user experience director and his team make all of our work useful, engaging and beautiful. I continue to feel lucky working with the extremely talented Float team. I wish us continued success.

I would like to thank Bradley University and its Interactive Media department. As an alumni and adjunct faculty, I have had the distinct pleasure to see the community there grow and evolve, never being content with complacency and ready to take on the next challenge.

My network of professionals in the learning space continues to inspire and challenge me. The eLearning Guild and ASTD are both great organizations to be part of. I cherish the time I get to spend with my cohorts there. There are so many, but here some of them that have made me think differently about what learning is: Aaron Silvers, Brent Schlenker, Reuben Tozman, Brandon Carson, Alicia Sanchez, Kris Rockwell, B.J. Schone, Justin Brusino, Cammy Bean, Jason Haag, Robert Gadd, Judy Brown and Clark Quinn. You all are quite inspiring. Thank you for the years of guidance and input. To all of my fellow "Up To All of Us"ers, wow. You push me to better myself. Thanks for being so good at what you do and thanks for all of the advice.

To my family and non-geek friends: Thank you for putting up with my "nerd talk" and ongoing obsession with mobile and technology. Finally, an acknowledgment of the impact that Steve Jobs had on my life. His vision really made all of this possible. I might have ended up an engineer or fulfilled my childhood dream of becoming a rock star (yeah, right) had it not been for SuperPaint, Strata3D, Hypercard, Apple Media Tool and all the nights spent hacking multimedia back in school.

Rock on.

ONE

UNDERSTANDING THE BENEFITS OF MOBILE LEARNING

And so, here we are. You've likely just gotten the word that you are going to start on a mobile learning project. Perhaps this project is a pilot or prototype. It could be a port of some existing content or a newly envisioned service for your employees. Maybe it's an enterprise-wide strategy. Congratulations! The first tough decision has been made.

There is no doubt that choosing to undertake mobile learning as an organization can be a daunting decision. Once you get past the initial decision to do it, the cold, harsh reality of what you have set out to do can start to set in. The questions arise. What now? How will I do this? Should I just convert my existing content to mobile? Is that even possible? Who on my team can help? What exactly am I going to produce? When will we know we are ready to launch? While you may have answers to some of these queries, it's rare that an organization will have the ability to answer most, let alone all, of these at the outset of implementing the mobile learning strategy.

In order to begin answering these questions, it's crucial that you first affirm your understanding of the many uses of mobile learning and what it can do for your organization. There are several new books on this topic available, such as Gary Woodill's *The Mobile Learning Edge*, or Clark Quinn's two books on this topic. From those readings, no doubt, you will learn that the power of mobile learning can be tremendous and freeing.

Consider, for a moment, your employees no longer tied to a desk or having to wait for a laptop to boot up to access that late-breaking recall notice. Or when they enter the job site, the most pertinent safety concerns could be made known to them. The very same device they use to call or send text messages can be the one they use to access company resources or knowledge. All this can be done from a touch-screen user interface or via text message (SMS) on a device you don't have to think about taking with you. There is never the question, "Well, should I pack this device for the trip today or not?" You simply take it with you.

Let's examine some of the high-level business benefits you should be considering for your mobile learning initiative. Hopefully you made note of some of these while you contemplated embarking on the journey. Perhaps they were whiteboarded with coworkers, scribbled on a napkin over a coffee or tea, or recorded in an Evernote notebook while in a meeting. If you haven't made such a list yet, please stop, put this book down for a moment, and do so. Think soundly about how you could see mLearning making a positive impact on your company. Then, when you are done, come back. Don't worry. I'll wait.

Great. You came back. I was worried there for a second. You may not have recorded them all, though, or perhaps you overlooked some of them. I have spent some time considering these, so let's take a look at some of the benefits. (Scribble any I missed in the sidebar here – it's your book; just go ahead and do it.)

- Increased Productivity
- Increased Sales
- Increased Accuracy
- Increased Connectivity
- Improved Communication
- Improved Attention to Detail
- Decreased Mistakes
- Decreased Defects
- Reduced Accidents
- Reduced Safety Incidents
- Reduced Risk
- Reduced Overall Cost of Learning
- Measurable return on investment (ROI)
- Increasing your overall activity levels by completing tasks done while on the go
- Accessing just-in-time information when it is needed
- Having easy access to colleagues and your personal learning network anywhere

Whew! Quite a list, right? I like the ones you added, by the way. Some are more provocative than others, no doubt. However, as someone who has to account for the value of the content you bring to your organization, if you could only accomplish even a third of these benefits on a routine project, I'm sure that you would have no problem getting management to sign off on any effort you led. It's plain to see that virtually all these factors lead directly to a measurable, bottom-line result. These are the kinds of things that you can print on a report and take to your management team so they will get behind your plan. You'll know you've succeeded because your learners will have succeeded. This is powerful stuff.

Let's take a look at the details for just a moment, shall we? Right off the bat, I mentioned increased productivity. Sure, that's an easy one. If you could put the right information in the right hands of the right person at the right time, wouldn't you be virtually assured that productivity has increased? It's possible to both create and show this with proper design, curation, deployment and measurement.

What about those increased sales? This is also easy to see. If your salespeople had a direct conduit to the latest competitive information bulletins right at their fingertips, the most pertinent details from the company's cavernous customer relationship management system, the very nuances of the objection the current customer is raising, wouldn't you be able to sell just about anything to your audience? Most likely, yes. If not, well, that's a different book.

And for increased accuracy? Check. No more guesses. A quick search of the company's mobile-friendly wiki makes the employee the smartest person in the room by knowing last quarter's numbers.

As far as connectivity goes, these devices were *made* for talking to other people. The very fabric of their existence is hinged around being able to connect people with the information and contacts that are needed at any given time. With around 1.2 billion 3G subscriptions globally as of October 2011 (*The World in 2011*, 2011, p. 4), and 4G coming on strong in many major markets, you are always just a swipe or click away from the information you need, so long as your content creators have made it available for mobile.

With connectivity comes communication. When there is no problem connecting with the content, and the device is in your hand to reach the source of that content or other subject matter experts (SME) in your personal learning network (PLN), why wouldn't you – in the vein of *Who Wants to Be a Millionaire?* – phone a friend? It makes perfect sense.

In my experience, coworkers who talk together produce together.

Colocation and improved attention to detail become a big deal when working on highly technical, difficult work. Certainly, ahead-of-time learning is important for this, but when your technician can access a manual for a piece of equipment without returning to the truck, or a fellow coworker forgets the sequence for an intricate testing process on the scene, what are you to do? Without the just-in-time delivery of this information, the work might go undone, or – maybe worse – it might be done incorrectly.

A decrease in mistakes is almost certain with mobile learning used this way. Imagine this: Several months ago, one of your employees worked her way through an eLearning module you created. But how can that employee access that same material on a smartphone or a tablet in a time of need? With mobile-ready content, that employee can always go back and refer to the important points of that training without having to sit through the entire module again. Curate, repackage and deploy, and see the number of recalls and elevated tech calls plummet.

Decreased defects would be great, right? Who wants to have to return to a recently implemented job simply to rework or replace a busted part or ruined piece? This sort of waste can be costly in terms of time, equipment, and logistics. With tools such as augmented reality or QR codes you can know that the right part is being used at the right time with near 100-percent certainty.

Beyond hardware issues, there is a human factor that is an important consideration. When you get a call from a dissatisfied customer
because something has gone wrong, your customer service reps often
have to save face by either calling up a tech to fix things or shipping a
replacement item. If you could augment your pick and pack lines via
mobile job aids or help your delivery staff stop accidentally shipping
the wrong part to the destination by having up to date information
available for them, you have just reduced waste.

If you ask any company with a mobile workforce what their
number-one priority is, it will inevitably be safety (perhaps after
some thought and maybe a little prodding), as accidents can result
in loss of time on the job due to injury. The cascading changes in
people's lives due to disability and the long-term effects thereof –
not to mention accidental death – can be avoided. Putting correct
information in a person's hand about changing job conditions, a
safety breach or other severe danger perhaps may be the only way to
prevent a catastrophe.

With reduced safety issues and accidents, your company's overall
risk profile is reduced. This is a number any accountant, actuary or
bean counter could love. It could be a trivial thing to fix, but it could
also have a significant financial impact. Now, that is power!

The 2011 ASTD State of the Industry Report makes it very clear
that training is getting more expensive to provide to everyone. The
overall amount of training being produced is going up. ASTD research-
ers found that the highest average volume of learning hours for BEST
Award-winning organizations – those the ASTD believes demonstrate
a clear link between learning and performance across the enterprise –
measured 56 hours per employee in 2010, the largest number since
ASTD began collecting data for this group. "The previous high average

was 47 learning hours in 2009," the ASTD reported, "also achieved by the BEST winners" (Green & McGill, 2011, p. 8).

In addition to this added content delivery and training content output, the overall reuse per hour of training is actually diminishing. From the report:

> The average direct expenditure per employee increased from $1,081 ($1,098 inflation adjusted) in 2009 to $1,228 in 2010. Overall, that represents nearly a 13-percent (11.8 percent inflation adjusted) increase in the amount spent per employee on learning and development. ... Despite the fact that the direct expenditure per employee increased in 2010, learning hours used per employee remained stable at 32 hours of formal learning content delivered per employee. (Green & McGill, 2011, p. 7)

This doing less with more approach is obviously not sustainable. There must be a disruptive action taken on our part as learning professionals if we are to shake this course. The use of next-generation learning techniques could very well be the disruption needed to shake the industry from its budgetary doldrums. That same report points out that for every one hour of mobile learning content available, there is only 1.5 hours of actual use.

ROI, or return on investment, is always tricky, no matter the industry. It's been the holy grail of training for a long time. It's often tough to measure reliably. Its true benefits are elusive and often not truly realized. Bemoaned and beatified at the same time, it is woefully misunderstood.

It comes down to this: if your current training – eLearning or otherwise – cannot be attached to a meaningful performance metric, how can you justify your workgroup's existence? Without this key piece of information, how can your content be adjusted to improve over time as the enterprise evolves?

Mobile learning cuts right to the chase. Because it is learning content applied at the point of need at the learner's request, it helps to get the work done. It tells the foreman that the situation has changed. It shows the technician how to do the job. It helps the sales person practice an activity or prepare for the meeting that lands the deal. Whether you are a behaviorism junkie, a cognitive enthusiast, or a humanist purist, you cannot argue with the fact that when the job is done with the information that you provide, you have succeeded. This is true ROI in its most evident form: actual results in the workplace. (Spoiler alert: I'll discuss ROI in greater depth in Chapter 4.)

So, then, how do you conjure up this powerful magic? How do you go about picking and choosing the most valuable content in your organization, and then formulate it into a digestible, usable nugget of mobile learning goodness? That's a big question and one with a multitude of answers and outcomes. There will be a lot of questions raised along the way that may cast a light on some of the bigger projects you've been doing in your company away from your smartphone (shh! I won't tell). What we need now, though, is a true method for reaching the end – the promised land of measurable ROI and the true worker: human performance improvement, or HPI. Yeah, I said it.

I know what some of you are thinking. "This isn't learning." This is simply a job aid or performance support. Believe me, as someone with more than a decade of experience in creating training materials, job aids, handouts, eLearning and presentation materials, I get that. I do. The point is that in some small ways I've stopped questioning myself on that. As learning professionals, members of a team, contributors to a common cause, isn't our true role to improve organizational performance by empowering our fellow employees?

This book, then, will serve as your blueprint for doing just that. Are you ready? Well, not so fast. First, we need to go over the strengths of mobile. How else can we be sure to use the best aspects of mobile and realize those elusive benefits we've been talking about?

ARTICULATING THE STRENGTHS OF MOBILE

Even with a large list of benefits such as those laid out already, it's still important not to overhype mobile learning. It can be great when implemented as part of a cohesive learning plan for your organization. It certainly is not, nor should it be, the end-all, be-all of training, learning or performance support. There are simply some matters that may not be best suited to mobile learning. After all, long-term learning is ultimately the goal of anyone dedicated to the art and science of teaching. As obviously pro-mLearning as I am, even I can admit that much and realize that mLearning is not the perfect solution in all cases. We must look at mLearning through the eyes of a critic. What can we truly accomplish when our workforce is mobile? Where will we see the biggest areas of improvement? What are the downsides to mobile learning?

It is useful to switch to the end users' points of view here. You will need to put yourself in their shoes, boots or galoshes to get a view of what they are doing in their day-to-day work. How do they see their tasks and the educational products you present to them? Are they prepared for their tasks? Do they have all the tools in front of them to do the job? Your ultimate goal is to empower them to make decisions and act independently, without fear of being incorrect or making mistakes, introducing defects, being too slow or getting hurt.

We aren't looking to replace the training content, remove ahead-of-time learning or do away completely with assessments. We are simply looking to ensure that nothing slips through the cracks.

Essentially, you are trying to augment your employees' knowledge. Let's look at some common ways a learner's knowledge base can be expanded in the field. David Metcalf explored these in his past writings, and Clark Quinn reviews them in his 2011 book *Designing mLearning*. The following is perhaps not an exhaustive – but certainly substantial – list of augmentations you can expect to employ:

- Supporting the learners in their environment;
- Supporting the learners in their preferred ways of learning;
- Adding pre-event and post-event learning;
- Giving just the right amount of content without overtraining;
- Taking into account the time aspect of context;
- Providing information with great currency;
- Providing information in bite-sized chunks that facilitate task completion; and
- Overlaying or providing a bit of metadata impossible without visualization.

Some heady topics there, huh? If you ever had a project that was focused on creating deliverables to be used by a learner at a point of need, most should be somewhat familiar to you. Others, such as pre-event learning and post-event follow-up have long been seen as desirable components to a blended learning curriculum. These seem a sure-fire way to measure both prerequisite competencies and long-term retention.

This approach to *slow learning*, a term coined by Clark Quinn, is in line with many current assertions about how the brain works.

John Medina in his book, *Brain Rules*, lays out arguments for why the brain is built for this kind of learning and, more importantly, how it actually leads to better long-term retention over the traditional classroom approach. To paraphrase Medina, people learn better for longer when the learning instances are smaller and spread out. Try doing that with classroom learning in today's distributed workforce, and you couldn't possibly support it. Put that content in a mobile-friendly format and see the consumption of learning materials skyrocket.

Many of these strengths might be more feature-rich when they are placed on a mobile device, but alone, with no improvement or re-imagining from their paper or laminate job-aid counterparts, you may find difficulty justifying the move to this new medium – the mobile device. You'll need to consider what makes this delivery method unique to get at the strengths of mobile learning. The addition of device sensors, easy connectivity, and advanced communication and data capabilities makes it possible to support the learners in their environment with a great deal of up-to-date information. You can make the right information available to the right person at the right time because of this added component – context.

You may feel the pinch in a few of these troublesome training areas right now. Perhaps tasks aren't getting done quickly enough. Maybe when it comes to serving your learners' diverse needs, there is too much of a one-size-fits-all approach that leaves some in the lurch. Providing an exhaustive list of content to everyone in a shotgun approach is a good way to spend your entire budget and still not have a good idea how it's being used.

On the subject of information currency, maybe your jobsite conditions change so frequently that a printout for the mobile technician created in the morning is out-of-date before lunch. Maybe the assembly process to install a part at a remote site is so complex that without seeing more detailed information about the placement, it's just not possible to install it in the amount of time needed to hit the efficiency metrics your management dictates. These sorts of real-world problems help to make the case for mobile learning pretty easy when you consider just how directly this kind of information delivery can impact productivity and accuracy.

In this respect, the real strengths of using mobile technology over even traditional job aids are manifold.

The reduction in printed materials is environmentally friendly. In 2011, United Continental Holdings announced the transition of printed pilot manuals into electronic formats for use on iPads. This action alone is expected to save 326,000 gallons of jet fuel by removing over 75 pounds of printed material from each airliner (*United Airlines Launches*, 2011).

Another key strength of mobile is the ease of maintenance going forward. Because of its portability, this is a great opportunity to free your content from the shackles of closed or proprietary LMSs or runtime plugins. With mobile learning solutions like OnPoint Digital's CellCast platform and the joint ADL/Scorm.com Project Tin Can effort, it is apparent that massive tidal shifts in how people deploy training are underway. Mobile can take advantage of these services, strengthening the position that learning takes place in the real world in addition to the classroom.

Because archaic distribution methods are being removed – after all, there are no more binders to ship – you can more rapidly deploy data to the learners and more frequently make minor adjustments with each subsequent release. This allows you to tune your messaging according to the analysis of performance reports and key metrics. Once you are no longer bound to quarterly booklets, shipping and fulfillment problems, and other foibles of traditional print, you can fix flubs such as typos, misprints and photos in flight. It takes only a simple command to publish your mobile learning content to the Web server, and all your learners will access new, accurate information the next time they use it.

Speaking of measurement, you can get detailed information on how your content is used and what your learners are doing with it. With the addition of true event-based analytics and usage information from platforms such as Adobe Captivate Companion, or time-tested analytics tools like WebTrends or Google Analytics, you'll be able to see just how your content is affecting performance.

Mobile learning strengthens real-time communication by virtue of the technology itself and the fact that these devices were made for it.

All these factors contribute to an overwhelming show of force for the team that decides to use mobile learning to enhance productivity and ultimately, profits. In mobile learning, we often do this through augmentation of information as needed rather than a prepared stand-alone presentation.

Whatever your need for the augmentation may be, mobile technology can help you reach your learners in nearly any setting imaginable today.

AUGMENTATION VS. PRESENTATION

All this talk of augmentation may be a bit foreign to some of you. What is it? How does augmentation differ from the traditional means of presentation? Is it really educational? The basic overall content of a presentation may also be used in the augmentation, so what is the true differentiator here?

The key lies in understanding the differences in the delivery methods, curation processes, and discovery paths the user employs to access content. Typical course content is generally presentational in nature. It's delivered in a read-only, ahead-of-time or just-in-case experience. Usually there is little need to refer to this material later, assuming that the learner has read the content, tried the exercises, and completed the assessments that are included in it. The learning has occurred and the learner is prepared and ready to use this new knowledge. That's a big assumption, I know. Because of the inevitable forgetting and the need for remediation, it's tough to see this type of experience being successful for anyone but the most attentive learners.

Presentational content is written from an authoritative stance, often containing the entire breadth of the topic so as not to miss anything in its delivery. After all, we may not know exactly when the learner may need or be able to refer to this content later, so we'd better give them everything, right? There is seldom an immersive tact taken to these lessons – you know, something that really lets the users see themselves in the setting and circumstances they are being trained to handle. While it's true that simulations or scenarios can be introduced, it's not often done via real-world role-playing in an actual situation or with interactivity in the truest sense.

Content is also usually delivered in a narrative or sequential form, taking the learners through the background information or setup, providing the introduction to the learning objectives, offering the learning module contents in a sequential form, and concluding the lesson with an assessment component.

Content is usually delivered as a push experience. There is really no discovery per se, since learning is part of the curriculum put forth by the organization. The content delivery's sequence is prescriptive. There is an order laid out because often one lesson leads to the next, building on the previous lesson, and provides new content that deepens the learners' understanding. The learners are aware of the content's availability because they are working with a scheduled training session, a piece of eLearning in an LMS, or a handout or job aid placed on the intranet or sent via email. The users don't seek out the content – it's distributed or presented by some source.

Augmentation, on the other hand, is meant to be and usually is delivered within the course of the activity. Today, it may be a laminated quick-reference card or a binder containing manuals. After you've gone through your mobile strategy, it could become a text messaging support system or an application enhanced by augmented reality (AR) that helps people identify the exact placement of components in the module they are servicing. The delivery takes place while in the situation they are encountering or the task they are performing. Only the most useful content is provided, because any extra content could be confusing to learners or prevent them from delivering a timely answer.

Augmentation makes people smarter, faster and more productive. It doesn't require taking them out of the flow of activity and instead strengthens them and sharpens their minds.

The content may come from an authority or a peer who has left a note on a knowledge base entry or posted a photo taken with his or her camera phone. The source, no matter what type it is, has been carefully culled down to the bare essentials that make it valuable. There is no filler and no need for extra user-interface niceties. It really is all about the content and ultimately makes for a superior user experience.

Augmentation and its delivery is not a push experience. Instead, it's usually a pull. After all, the learner needs this content – hence the request. The learner is looking for a specific piece at a particular time in a discrete situation. This is that person's context. It determines the content that he or she needs, and as the situation unfolds, he or she can communicate with the system used to obtain the most likely or useful information. There is no sequence needed because that information is a singular bit of knowledge to be used at an equally singular moment. The only scheduling of content is by virtue of the worker's daily routine.

These are two sides of the same coin – each equally important.

IN SUMMARY

There are many benefits to and strengths of mobile learning. Everything from increased productivity and ROI to decreased safety issues or wasteful processes can be the outcome for a successfully crafted mobile learning experience. It is crucial for any sufficiently mature and thoroughly thought-out strategy that mobile learning has a solid foundation in these benefits and strengths. In order to deploy augmentation properly for your learners, you must capitalize on these traits to create a great pull experience, using curated content delivered at the point of need.

Any less is not enough. Any more is waste. You will need a content strategy to make sure you nailed it.

TWO

FINDING MOBILE LEARNING OPPORTUNITIES AND DETERMINING HOW TO FILL THEM

IDENTIFYING AUDIENCE NEEDS

Because a user's context is important and you will often be augmenting existing learning to deliver it at the point of need, you must have a solid understanding of the audience. You have to know and understand their needs, their constraints, their work roles, the devices they carry and how they use them. All these need to be taken into account before embarking on the path to putting mobile content in their hands.

Deploying mLearning is not an insignificant undertaking, but it can be accomplished with some smaller steps to help you break up the work. You may have access to some human resources reporting that can help with basic demographics. Your IT department may be able to provide technology profiles and usage data that can help you with understanding the current IT structure. Your training colleagues may be able to offer some basics on content usage and needs in the organization. If you operate in a structure that employs content developed by contract workers or deals with franchising situations, it can be tough to access this information and in some cases may not be possible to do at all.

There are some mechanical or automated routes to take that will help with this. The use of Web analytics and reports that outline usage of the content from websites, LMSs and intranets can provide a great deal of intelligence on the types of content that resonate with your user base. With reverse IP address and geolocation analytics, you can get an idea of where your users are accessing your content as well. These are not silly parlor tricks. A content strategy that takes these considerations into account can be powerful.

This sort of basic, bland method to user analysis can seem a bit cold or inconsistent with the premise that mobile learning should be just-in-time, just-the-right-size and just-for-me. We'll be getting to a deeper

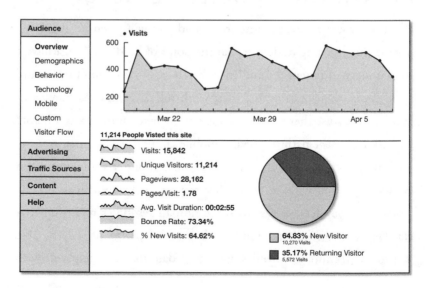

examination of user behavior and heuristics in a bit, but first, a bit on the advantages of this slightly detached approach.

By coming at this analytically, it will be more apparent which content is the must-have information for your efforts. You will be more likely to hit the mark with the content you choose. It will be easier to cut what you don't need. You will be able to respond to inquiries about your work because you know you did your due diligence.

An important note: Do not mistake a lack of mobile traffic or usage of a specific piece of content you know would be valuable to users for lack of interest or usefulness. Check the page or site on your device. Is it just so poorly designed as to be completely useless on your targeted device profiles? If so, obeying analytics in this case is how you create a self-fulfilling prophecy. Is the Field of Dreams real? If you build it, will they come?

The only way to know is to dig deeper. Surveys can help with that.

SURVEYING AND GETTING INPUT

Ahh, the survey! I'm sure you've been on a team that created one or two of these in the past, right? As begrudged as they might be, it's unlikely that this type of resource-gathering for a strategy project is going to go away anytime soon. A survey is just about the easiest way to get a pulse on the group of people for whom you are trying to craft a solution. If they are well assembled and delivered unobtrusively, you can get the information you need and not worry about inconveniencing your colleagues.

The survey you produce can be done in any number of ways, be it in person, via an online questionnaire, or even over the phone. The method used is not important; the content and the results are.

You need a significant number of responses to make informed decisions in your design process. How many is that? Does it need to be a statistically significant number? Very likely, no. If you can get a good cross section of the team you are serving, that may be good enough. How many people is this? The answer will vary depending upon your situation. The more people you are targeting, the more people you should survey. Will 5 percent or 10 percent percent of your audience suffice? It's quite possible that it will. Some of the initial results will provide good picture of how many people you need to evaluate. After all, you are looking to uncover pain points, not preferences. An exhaustive market survey that enables multi-variable testing would be nice but is likely not required for a first pilot or proof-of-concept effort to test your theories.

Here are some sample questions you could use in your survey to reach the core of what your users need to do and what they expect from your team in terms of a mobile effort:

- What is the primary mobile device you use for communication today? (Choose one.)
    - A simple cell phone (non-smartphone)
    - An iPhone
    - An Android smartphone
    - A BlackBerry smartphone
    - A Windows 7 smartphone
    - Other (please name)

- Would you use company information, training or performance support materials on your phone if they were made available to you today?

- Do you currently use your phone to do any of the following?

(Check all that apply.)
- Browse for information on the Web
- Watch videos
- Play games
- Use social media websites and apps
- Use apps for finance, home management or other complex tasks
- Text message (SMS)
- Send emails
- Use voice communications
- Find directions or use maps

- How do you prefer to get information to help you with your job now?
  - Ahead-of-time training (such as instructor-led or eLearning)
  - Calling on colleagues for guidance
  - Take-along handouts or other job aids
  - Referring to company resources like knowledge bases or wikis.
  - Other

- Name the three most commonly used apps on your smartphone.
  - -
  - -
  - -
  - N/A (I don't have a smartphone.)

- Do you have a tablet device?

- Do you find the tablet device easier, more difficult or about the same amount of difficulty to use as your computer?
  - Easier

- ■ More difficult
- ■ About the same

- What is something you can remember learning while using your mobile device?

- Complete this sentence: "I think that smartphones and tablets are _____".

- Are your customers and/or vendors using smartphones to communicate, gain information and do business functions?

- What job function would you like to make easier by having help from a tablet or smartphone?

Your actual questions may vary, but these will help you get going in the right direction.

What is your primary mobile device you use for communication today?

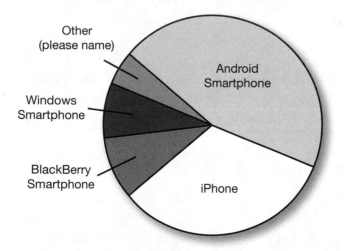

Note: Hypothetical results for an organization.
Based on aggregated industry numbers.

What we're seeking are major trends in the content the users need for their day-to-day work. Are there common job functions that are causing bottlenecks? Maybe some tasks or items are frequently overlooked or missed during a typical day. These types of trends are what we should note while analyzing the survey.

Here are some tips for creating the survey:

- Keep it short – more than 10-12 questions is too many.

- Make your questions count. You'll likely only get one shot at this, so run your questions by a coworker or two.

- Use quantifiable answers for at least half your survey. You need something on which to hang your hat here. Too many touchy-feely questions will give you too little to build upon.

- When you send out your survey, make sure everything is good to go. You don't want to scramble to fix issues while in flight. Doing so will make validating your findings nearly impossible (plus it makes you look like a bit of a goof).

- Give an incentive, if possible. A $10 gift card (or sometimes just the chance to win one) goes a long way to encourage participation.

- Be sure to let people know the time-sensitive nature of your survey. Give them a deadline to complete it and stick to that.

Beyond surveying, how else can you get input from your team members? Depending on company policies and your availability, you may be able to job-shadow some of your mobile coworkers. Log their technology usage and pain points while they are away from the desk. When are they reaching for their phone or laptop? Are they spending a lot of time negotiating a network connection with a laptop? What frustrates them about the materials you have already supplied? How many of them have lost the job aids you thought they depended upon?

A day or two away from your desk would be a good thing. Not only can you skip that weekly status meeting, but you can also have some face time with your learners and hear directly from them what really makes their day tough. You'll see everything in a whole new light. Not only will you have a better idea of how your content gets used, you'll be able to spot gaps in your curriculum and possibly even win over a potential beta tester or two for your pilot efforts.

So, got your survey out? Great. Got the results back? Not yet... Still waiting on that guy from marketing, aren't you? Ugh. That guy.

Well, while we wait for the results to come in, let's turn our gaze outward.

What are others doing in the space we share? Are our competitors nailing it, or are they absent from the scene?

COMPETITIVE RESEARCH AND POSITIONING

Market forces are certainly at play in the consumer space. The mobile industry is growing faster than ever before. The number of smartphones selling continues to skyrocket. Apps in the markets and stores number in the millions. The downloads are staggering. Surely, your competitors must be there. Are you too late?

I wouldn't count on it. According to analysis of a 2011 Tim Cook transcript from 2011, 93 percent of Fortune 500 companies are testing or deploying on iPhone. That's just 60 percent of the Global

500 (Hesseldahl, 2011). Jumping into the marketplace because your competitors are there wouldn't necessarily be the best strategy anyway. If they are there, you'll need to pay close attention to what they are doing. Are they offering basic sales data and marketing collateral or something more? A silly throwaway application wouldn't be in your best interest anyway. Actually, building an app just to get something out there that offers little value or reason for re-launching could be detrimental to your brand. Flurry, a mobile analytics firm, revealed statistics in October 2011 that may get you to think about your potential app. According to their findings, within less than a month of initially downloading and using the app, less than half of users continued using it. After four months have passed, the number drops to 1 in 5, and after a year, 1 in 20 (Farago, 2011). Your messaging, look, and feel must reflect the other materials you are producing. Doing anything less would cheapen your brand.

That is certainly true for publicly released applications, but what about the ones you don't see? You know, the applications deployed behind enemy lines, the ones behind a firewall or VPN that are used by employees to access company data. According to Kony's Second Annual Mobile Marketing and Commerce Study released in September 2011, 71 percent of Fortune 500 companies are in the planning or early stages of launching their mobile offerings, a 15-percent increase over their 2010 survey. However, "only 10 percent of brands have fully deployed all aspects of their mobile offering, a decrease of 3 percent from 2010" (Kony Solutions, 2011, p. 4). Even though companies are mostly able to find funding, Kony said that "brands are unable to rapidly deploy full offerings to the range of devices, channels and variety of features and functions available" (Kony Solutions, 2011, p.

4). Even though companies are mostly able to find funding, Kony said that "brands are unable to rapidly deploy full offerings to the range of devices, channels and variety of features and functions available." Therefore, as you can see, you probably aren't too late for the party at all. In fact, you may be arriving at just the right time. You've got time to do a little searching to find out what your vertical market looks like, and likely are not so late that you cannot claim a leadership position with your first successful mobile learning effort.

This window may be closing, though. The ASTD reported in its 2011 Mobile Learning report that 57.2 percent of organizations plan within the next three years to design learning programs so mobile devices can access them. Further, mobile learning continues to grow, according to Ambient Insight's research,

> The US market for mobile learning products and services reached $958.7 million in 2010. The five-year compound annual growth rate (CAGR) is 13.7% and revenues will reach $1.82 billion by 2015. (Adkins, 2011, p. 5).

> The US is now the top-buying country of mobile learning, followed by Japan, South Korea, the UK, and Taiwan. Combined, these five countries accounted for 69.8% of the total 2010 global mobile learning market. This dynamic is changing fast. By 2015, these five countries will only account for 40.6% of all expenditures. The highest growth rates are in China, India, Indonesia, and Brazil. By the end of the forecast period, China will be the second largest buying country after the US. (Adkins, 2011, p. 5).

By 2015, it's likely that virtually all companies will be doing some amount of mobile learning or performance support on mobile devices. You can guess this means the productivity of your competitors is about to go up. All this augmentation is bound to help a few of them, right?

Will you be ready to deliver a well-thought-out strategy and pilot in time to meet that challenge? It's a good thing you are doing a bit of research now, rather than later.

Competitive research isn't necessarily a "keeping up with the Joneses" kind of thing so much as a "we're keeping our eye on you" kind of thing. You should be mindful, not fearful. Use this intelligence to guide your efforts and make a case to either maintain positioning in your space or establish leadership in your market. When you can find concrete evidence of the leaders in your market space working in the mobile area, public or otherwise, you can bet that some mobile learning efforts are underway there as well. The old adage is that if you see one mouse, then you probably have ten mice. In the app world, you can bet that if there is a publicly available app for a company's brand in marketing, then someone in their training department has begun efforts to move some learning content over to mobile as well.

You will probably see some efforts your competitors are undertaking that aren't very well thought-out or are lacking polish in execution. This is an opportunity to improve on the work that's been done and learn from their mistakes. Think of it as the best worst pilot you never had to pay for.

You may need to turn your attention back to your company and the work ahead of you. Hopefully, you have all those surveys back now. We need to do a bit of digging in our content library. Surely we have something we can prepare for a quick proof of concept to try out mobile learning on a scale that won't break the bank but still lets us test our proposed approach.

LEVERAGING CONTENT AND CONCEPTS IN YOUR LIBRARY

Sometimes when people embark on something new, they feel they need to begin from scratch. While it can be nice to get a fresh start from time to time, it can also be expensive – all new asset creation, subject matter expert (SME) interviews, content writing, and all the other activities you need to complete for any learning project take time. The same holds true with instructor-led training, eLearning, and social or mobile learning.

That said, you probably have a wealth of content you can leverage to put together something quickly. What types of content seem to resonate with your audience the most? Which of those messaging opportunities are best suited for mobile? Which of these are the most polished and have the best media assets like photos, illustrations, videos and animations? These are where you want to focus your attention.

When starting to go mobile, you need to give yourself solid footing. Picking a module from a long-forgotten and often-resented mandatory compliance curriculum wouldn't exactly put you in a sure-fire win stance, would it? It would launch, you'd have less-than-stellar results, then what? You would have taught your learners that mobile is no fun and offers little improvement over your existing efforts in eLearning. There goes your budget for next year. Don't look to take a stinker and turn it into gold in a brand-new delivery method. Just like the scientific method needs a control group in order to be properly employed, a pilot program should have one or options that should be tested.

With some quick quantitative research from your LMS and the analytics you have in place, you can see where the highest levels of utilization lie. Which pieces of content are most frequently used? Which ones have the highest reuse per hour of training? Which ones are the most frequently retried? Are the learners seeing improved results with reuse? If any of these courses are applicable to a mobile audience, flag them for later follow-up. You may want to consider moving this content to mobile in some form. That is not to say that you will want to port it over directly, but perhaps some of the content should be tried on a mobile audience.

You may also have some smile sheets available in your LMS depending on your implementation. Which courses have the best feedback going right now? Which ones have gotten you the most inquiries regarding their ability to provide related job aids? If you are getting decent feedback in your existing systems, it would be a great time to act on it as you move to mobile. People aren't often that great at telling you exactly what they want, but they are usually pretty good at identifying their problems and areas where they can see room for improvement.

Learning departments don't stay still for long. Odds are that you have a number of efforts underway to redesign or rework some of your existing courseware library. In the coming year, which of your old stalwarts will get a refresh? What were some common issues with that course or those courses? Maybe there are ways to bring that content to a mobile audience and turn it into a winner. We'll get down to brass tacks on how to do just that in a bit, but for now, make a mental note to ask your coworkers about upcoming projects in the department.

Looking outside of the typical L&D realm, what key initiatives are other groups lining up in the business at large? Are any mobile projects or strategy working groups shaping up? Better poke your head in and get involved. If there is new software or processes in development, you can bet new training will be needed. If these applications or services are to be performed or used away from the typical office setting you may want to offer up a tag-along mobile learning effort to ensure a successful launch for everyone.

IN SUMMARY

In order to provide contextual learning via augmentation, you will need to understand the context of the learner. This can be done in a variety of ways. Using mechanical analytics, you can gather quite a bit of up-front data about the existing libraries' overall usages. While this is useful information, it should not be considered the only way to learn about your users. You should consider conducting a survey to dig deeper. Another great way to get the information you want is through the in-person analysis of learner behaviors.

Outside your area, you should analyze what others in the space are doing with mobile. This basic competitive research may turn up some great information that you can use to improve your project. Many companies are just getting into this as well, so there is still time to establish your organization as a leader in mobile learning.

Before lining up your efforts, think of the bigger picture – about the content that you already have. Which stones are about to be over-turned? Are there ways to re-imagine some of this content for use in a mobile-learning effort? Maybe this soft reset you are about to under-take is a great opportunity to integrate your efforts with others in the organization who are also investigating mobile options.

THREE

WHAT IS CONTENT STRATEGY AND HOW DOES IT APPLY TO MOBILE LEARNING?

A PLAN FOR CONTENT

Content strategy is not a new concept. First coming up in advanced Web design circles in the late 1990s, then rising to prominence in the mid-2000s as a way to increase meaningful, long-term user engagement and also prevent site burnout or editorial fatigue, it is a discipline with a long history – that is, a long history outside of learning circles.

You see, we learning professionals are a funny bunch – perfectionists, cerebral, maybe a bit dictatorial. We see a need for content, a gap, and we fill it rather than rework it. Rather than tweak to meet the missed objectives, we're completely content with throwing the bathwater out, the baby and – hey, why not? – the tub, too. I've seen courses suffering from overly obtuse interactions that are entirely trashed because learners didn't get it, and so the instructional designers or the business partners believed they missed the mark and needed to reboot. I've been on projects to come in and replace enterprise LMSs because learners weren't engaged when faced with what was probably a usability or accessibility issue, not a real problem with the learning itself. This is also done under the auspices of improving end-user experience or maybe organization change, but in reality, it's hard for me to see this as anything but waste. This is waste in the purest sense and from virtually all aspects of measurement – money, time, and effort.

The sort of waste caused by a lack of goals and overall planning can be eliminated when switching to mobile learning. At the very least, it can be significantly reduced by choosing a content strategy then executing it. This can be a difficult undertaking, though, not to be entered into by mere mortals. What, first of all, is a content strategy? Glad you asked.

From the slightly more progressive and agile Web design community, we can get a great definition of content strategy. Kristina Halvorson writes:

> Content strategy plans for the creation, publication and governance of useful, usable content. (Halvorson, 2008).

Now, let's take a look at that, shall we? "Creation, publication and governance." We'll cover these in depth in the next few chapters, but first, we'll get a good overview of each part before diving in. For years as learning professionals, we've been doing something similar to content strategy at the outset of a learning strategy effort, only we call it *curriculum development*. The prescriptive nature of curriculum development – the what, how, and when learning will be delivered – is in many ways akin to some key elements in content strategy. Again, from Halvorson:

At its best, a content strategy defines:

- key themes and messages,
- recommended topics,
- content purpose (i.e., how content will bridge the space between audience needs and business requirements),
- content gap analysis,
- metadata frameworks and related content attributes,
- search engine optimization (SEO), and
- implications of strategic recommendations on content creation, publication, and governance. (Halvorson, 2008).

Overall, it's comparable to the elements in the curriculum for your organization, right? Extrapolate a few of those bullet points to be applied to learning content, and we are looking at a systemic (or *deeply ingrained in the system*), systematic (or *carried out using step-by-step processes and procedures)* approach to delivering content to our learners. The *what* we are going to teach is covered; we have the purpose in mind, and the topics are aligned with that purpose. The *how*, or the means by which we are going to reach our audience, is addressed; the messaging is defined and we know the mode in which the content will be delivered, whether it be instructor-led, eLearning, blended, social or now, mobile. The *when* is also apparent, as the end goal is articulated and the metadata tells us the context in which it should be relayed. This could be at a scheduled training session, an apprentice/mentoring session, on-the-job training, a company eLearning lab, someone's desk, or now with mobile, just about any of these. The content's perceived qualities, purpose and values are made known to the learners at the outset via stated learning objectives in the course and expectations. The content is made accessible to all regardless of conveyance. The ongoing stewardship of this content is planned at the beginning, not at the time of deployment.

When fully realized, this content-strategy model works across a variety of modalities. You can begin to see that simply saying, "Mobile learning is cool and we should do it," is woefully inadequate. The knee-jerk reaction elicited by the many television commercials that say, "We need an app for that," is anathema to a content strategy for mobile. The search for the eLearning-to-mLearning-conversion easy button is a fool's errand when seen in this light.

Adherence to this content strategy is not easy. It will take discipline. Easy-to-use tools, limited budgets and aggressive timelines might push you to make some rash decisions. You may already have the hoards knocking down the gates! Do this: Make them wait for the app they think they need. Tell them that you need to assess the situation, and that converting the courseware may not be adequate and could lead to waste or perceived failure to meet the learners' needs. If that doesn't work, throw something shiny in the other direction while you get back to work. That ought to hold them for a while.

THE IMPORTANCE OF A CONTENT STRATEGY

Now that you know what a content strategy is, can you see the value in having one? While it's possible to sketch out a basic overview of what you might like to achieve with your learning curriculum then just go for it, you will likely end up making quite a few mistakes. These are the kinds of errors that could have been avoided with a bit more upfront critical thinking about how the material you're going to produce will be consumed and how it will add to the overall learning of the individual and the organization. This sort of *just enough* analysis and strategy is a tough line to walk. How will you know when you have considered enough possibilities, but not over-thought them?

A key to knowing this is having access to your existing content and being able to assess its overall value. In the previous chapter, I asked you to take a look at your library to see what you have. When considering taking it to mobile, there are some matters to keep in mind. You will need to look at the roles for which you intend to train and catalog the content you have for these roles. Some key questions you'll want to ask yourself are:

- What content exists for your typically mobile users?

- What content is currently missing?

- Which pieces of content have been the most effective?

- Which pieces of content have failed?

- Are the content pieces currently in use?

- Have some pieces of content fallen into disuse because of their perceived lack of value?

- When was the last time the content was updated?

- Is the content still accurate from a messaging standpoint? What about branding? Is it still factual?

- Is the SME, writer or original author available for questions?

- Who owns the content?

- How is the content currently cataloged and organized?

- What derivatives of this content currently exist?

- Is this content easily searchable?

- Is the content scrapeable (able to be pulled from the current source and reused)?

- Does a clean, normalized form of this content exist that would be useful in a re-imagining of it?

- Are there short forms or job aids based on this content already available?

You need to answer a good portion of these questions, or you may not be thinking holistically enough about your content. Because you probably have a mobile-learning version of the content already in use, the need is not truly burning down the house. Hopefully, the barbarians are not at the door with torches and pikes, so take your time, analyze and concisely report to your team on your library's content status. You need to move quickly, of course, but you should also be sufficiently thorough so that if you are later questioned about your approach or need to readjust to meet new demands, you will have a historical analysis and information to back up your choices that let people know you did your homework. These questions do not need scads of data for each project, but you should have a simple case or cases for your plan that help your outside stakeholders or business partners understand where you are coming from with your recommendations.

This analysis should take into account the process that we will use in recreating, distributing, and ultimately managing and maintaining the content for sustainable deployment across multiple platforms. Remember, we are moving outside the usual learning and development comfort zone in some regards. If you are familiar with eLearning, then you're likely used to developing one authoritative version of your content that is delivered to all learners. This one-size-fits-all approach doesn't usually work so well in the mobile realm, so you are going to have to readjust your thinking. Tablet users and mobile phone users each have different capabilities and needs. Android users have a different interface and experience expectations than iOS users. BlackBerry devices are often not as fast or advanced as many top-tier smartphones are. Windows and Nokia devices are sometimes marginalized, but you will also need to address these if they represent a significant percentage of your user base.

The process you are undertaking is a broader and more detailed than what might be considered typical work for a Web team. You are looking not only at the types of mobile content across a number of job functions, but also their overall effectiveness as a learning tool to gain expertise in an area.

Because producing compliance or safety-learning content often has legal implications involved in its approval process and ongoing auditing, we must be pragmatic and careful to ensure that all users, regardless of device class or use case, can have easy access to the most critical information. You cannot omit something because a user's device doesn't have a camera or the screen size is too small.

The content strategy for mobile also must look at the modality used for delivery as a vital part of its composition. When people use an app as opposed to a mobile website, they respond to content differently. Images and video in a media player framework are not used and referred to in the same ways as non-visual content. SMS and MMS, email and other messaging formats such as BlackBerry Messenger, instant messages and iMessages are also quite different as a content conveyance and have differing levels of immediacy and desired responses. Automated call centers, knowledge bases, smart user agents and systems of that nature also carry with them some inferred user activities and proclivities. Perhaps "the medium really is the message," to quote Marshall McLuhan.

Do some of these modalities better match up with your company's culture than others? Only you will be able to determine that. Hopefully some information gained during your surveying and shadowing activities will shed some light on this.

As you can see, the naive statement that started all this talk in the first place – "We need an app!" – is just a bit laughable in hindsight now. We're talking about not only designing a great experience here, but understanding why and how it will be created, where and when it will be distributed, and who will maintain it and what the long-term health of it looks like.

CREATION OF CONTENT

After inventorying your content and surveying, you have likely found some trends you can use to begin forming ideas on what is needed to move to mobile. With these building blocks out on the table, we can begin the blueprinting stage in the content creation process.

We will need to take the information to sit down with our content creators, writers, SMEs, designers and developers. Then we should identify what must stay in the content library and what will migrate to the mobile format to support the basic overall learning objective as well as strengthen the selected content. We will also need to pinpoint the unnecessary elements that should be left out or pushed to a second phase of the release.

We should be looking at what sorts of programmatic elements are going to be reworked to fit this new engine or delivery platform. Odds are whatever you used to build these products the first time around is not going to be the same toolkit you use to deliver for mobile. With a wide variety of desktop publishing tools, rapid eLearning development tools and mobile software development kits, that would be far too convenient. Don't let this be a source of worry, though. If you could simply re-compile your learning content for mobile, would your learners even like it? Consider the various ways you interact with websites or platforms such as Facebook, Twitter, Flickr, CNN. com, Netflix or Amazon. Every one of those companies has a different experience for the users based on the device they use to access the content. An app is different from a set top box, which is also different from the Web browser, which is different from the mobile Web. These experiences weren't created by pumping their respective sites through a magic transformer of sorts. Some features are omitted or tucked away as they may be unneeded in a particular case, but the key functions the user requires in that particular case – desktop, Web, mobile, etc. – are accounted for and designed.

So, too, will your carefully crafted mobile learning experience account for these platforms. Running your Flash course through some sort of HTML5 mill is not the answer. You must redesign and adapt your applications to fit within your content strategy for mobile. Beyond the basic considerations you must take into account, such as user interface element size and scale, there are some more dramatic shifts you will need to make in your thinking.

For years we have done whatever we could to make our learning engaging, beautiful and immersive. Sometimes this has worked well; other times, not so much. Some features that spring to mind are overly long or dramatic animations and introduction sequences, gimmicks such as walk-on avatars, and extremely elaborate or ornate user interfaces. These are often the by-product of a design by a committee, and rarely do they contribute to better learning. In mobile, these contrivances are death. No one is going to hunt and peck through an app interface to find the content. People barely put up with this sort of thing in a required eLearning environment. In mobile, where you are competing with the outside world and are only one or two touches away from being dumped in favor of a session of *Angry Birds*, you must provide instant access to valuable content.

Some of this content from your original software may stay largely in tact. I can imagine a thoroughly indexed and well-manicured company wiki may require only a new mobile theme and perhaps the addition of some basic contextual awareness to make it a valuable mobile learning tool. Other items – like immersive software simulations, for example – may require more thought prior to porting the content to iOS or Android handsets. These devices do have constraints in terms of screen size, bandwidth and processing power, and in order to match the experience to the target platform, you may have to take these into account in your design process.

On the topic of conversion to mLearning from eLearning, I am split. While, yes, it's great to be free to leverage your content and repackage it for a new class of users in need of it, none of the simple paths to mobile learning I have seen truly put the *mobile* into the design up front. They may apply a new mobile-friendly skin to the content, sure, but that's the easy way out. Seldom do I hear of learners impressed by its content delivery. On the other hand, I constantly hear people impressed by Urbanspoon's scope feature, Facebook's streamlined feel on smartphones, or Twitter's ease of uploading images or adding location data to posts. This sort of smart user experience design, to which we as consumers have grown accustomed, takes work. If page-turning eLearning was a sure-fire way to create *snoozeware* on the desktop, then it's death on the mobile side.

Remember, by and large, we are **not** looking to replace – or even directly replicate – the experience that people have when interacting with learning content on their personal computers or even sitting in a full classroom setting with an instructor. This content should not just be recompiled or republished. You will need to examine its design and cut the extra content, chrome and waste then use that reduced weight to craft a focused, well-thought-out effort.

In Chapter 5, "Key Content Types for Mobile Learning," we will go over some innovative ways to repackage and repurpose your content to prevent that most horrible fate of any mobile app – its removal from the user's home screen. First, let's talk about how we are going to get our repackaged information into the learner's hands.

DISTRIBUTION OF CONTENT

It's a great idea to lay out a clear plan of how the deployment of your content is going to happen before you begin the full-on design and development effort used to produce it. Your organization may have some policies in place that could hold up this step, so thinking ahead pays off. There are a lot of misconceptions about how mobile content has to be pushed out to users. Some of my favorites are:

- Setting up SMS is tough.

- Using SMS is expensive.

- We need to use our LMS to track other content.

- You can't track usage of an app as easily as you can courseware.

- Apps have to go through the Apple App Store.

- Mobile devices aren't secure.

- The learners bring in their own devices, so we can't put company information on them.

- Company policy prevents us from using mobile devices at work.

- Using (insert product here) as a development tool for apps is a surefire way to get your app rejected.

- Our users aren't smart enough to put apps on their devices.

- We have BlackBerry devices – they can't do anything.

Let's cover these on a case-by-case basis. I'm sure you'll see there are a lot of distribution options for mobile. Let's keep in mind after all that this isn't rocket science or brain surgery. Would either of those make good subjects for mobile learning? Hmmm...

Using text messages, or SMS, in your mobile learning is not difficult, and it doesn't have to be expensive. Most major SMS providers have some easily accessible Web application programming interfaces (APIs). If you have a reasonably savvy Web developer on your staff or available to you who can program WordPress, SharePoint, Drupal or any number of common and Web-capable content management systems, then you can usually cobble together a pretty functional Web-powered SMS system in short order. Much of the dilemma springs from people not having a good grasp of how the process works and how a Web service functions. Since it's not visual, it really is a purely programming/development matter. Put your content into a CMS that supports a Web service layer. Create a database query layer that retrieves data based on your inquiries, then a couple application flow diagrams. Give your developer access to a few knowledge base articles

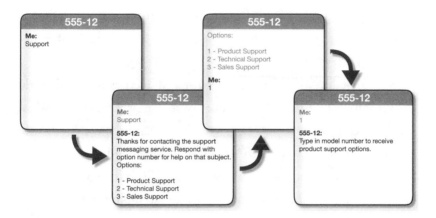

and PDF manuals, and you might just have something there. Check out this diagram for a basic SMS-based technical support application:

Most SMS carriers are well below $0.05 USD per message and have advanced features like sticky sessions. If you are not in need of a private short code, this can be quite economical to configure. You may need to pay $15,000+ for a custom or private short code, but if you **really** need one of those, you can probably afford it, too. I have had some success negotiating SMS vendors down from their published price based on volume and length of contract. It's always worth a call to see if they can do something for you.

There is a bit of a tidal shift underfoot regarding LMS usage. While LMS packages are great and serve a real purpose for tracking compliance and other baseline metrics, there have been some sharp criticisms that as the workforce has become increasingly mobile, there has been a shortcoming in tracking real-world performance and results. Few, if any, LMS implementations are so integrated with business process systems such as CRM, ERP or other enterprise software that you would be able to draw a direct correlation between performance in the courseware and performance on the job. Even if you could, correlation is not causation. Therefore, because performance is not directly tied to ahead-of-time learning content, truly measuring ROI is not possible anyway.

With mobile, Web analytics, event-based metrics and real-world conversions – Did the job get done? Was it finished correctly? Is it on time? Did everyone stay safe? etc. – You can accurately, down to minutes and meters, tell when tasks were finished and how. Does this fit in line with your LMS measurements? No, but maybe it's time to challenge those. Inserting analytics into an application is a trivial matter; it integrates similarly to how you do it with Web pages. You can track views, users, conversion points, assessments and anything else you normally would in your LMS.

You may not believe this, but you can deploy applications to your colleagues without pushing your content through an app store. I recently came across a 500+ MB application in the Apple App Store that was a proprietary sales aid application. This is for a major brand that a number of people like, follow and are loyal to. The scenario was this: You needed to download the application, wait – mind you, this was a biggie – and have it fill your device's precious storage (internal flash storage is currently going for $100 per 16 GB on tablets). Then, when you launched the application, it asked for a username and password, and unless you were a company employee, you didn't have one. Seems like an exercise in futility to me.

This could have been circumvented with some planning. Android already allows deployment without submitting your app to Google Play. BlackBerry has the BlackBerry Enterprise Server. Apple has something similar to this in the Enterprise Developer Program. For $299 per year, you can deploy your applications to an unlimited number of devices used by your organization's employees with no extra fees nor approval needed from the Apple App Store review staff. Shocking news, I know. Once you have signed up for this program, it's not readily apparent how you can put your apps in the hands of your users. The bottom line is that you can publish your apps to any HTTPS-enabled Web server and upload your IPA file for download. It's not that difficult, but perhaps a bit beyond your typical department's jurisdiction, and maybe even its capabilities. After all, in the corporate world, Web space isn't always so free and easy to come by.

For those of you in this situation, do not despair. There are a number of emerging vendors in the mobile device management (MDM) and mobile application management (MAM) spaces that you can use to get your apps out to your learners without publicly publishing your apps, requiring your Android users to jump through hoops, or requiring your iOS users to visit a Web page – so low-brow, right? – in order to add your content to their devices. These typically subscription-based or SaaS-based solutions allow you to publish your apps to the cloud on your own accord then permit your users to install the apps without needing an app store account.

These solutions are pretty slick. Many of them allow you to push other content such as video, DOC, XLS, and PDF files. In addition, you can also require certain security settings to be enabled to access the content inside, meaning you can secure previously unsecure devices. Whether the company or the person owns the equipment, by sharing a bit of software between the company and the user you can deploy applications to the device and remove them if an employee loses his or her position or moves to another role in the company. Very nice, indeed! I'm not sure how many birds you may have killed with that stone, but it was probably a few.

Using some tough love can make your devices a lot more secure when deployed. Do you currently require pass codes on your devices? No? Well, you can. Do you enforce auto-timeout and device locking? No? It's possible. Do you have a device or application-level remote data process in place? No? This is now a possibility as well.

It may not be as readily apparent to you or your team how to do this because you haven't been dealing with this problem as long as you have typical desktop PC security issues, but most typical security scenarios that arise have been taken care of, and then some. Device-level encryption? Check. Brute force password protection? Check. Secure Wi-Fi data transfer? Check. The list goes on. If persons in your organization are stonewalling based on assumptions they have from two or more years ago, then they need to go read some newer documentation. Let's remember this: the mobile world changes quickly. We are no longer beholden to a three or four-year PC desktop replacement schedule. Operating systems and devices come out monthly. Entire platforms are upgraded in a year. This isn't your uncle's IT landscape anymore.

Take a look at how mobile operating systems are advancing in

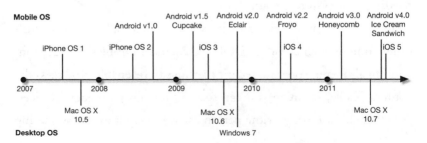

comparison to the same desktops OSs. You'll notice that mobile OSs are advancing at a much quicker pace.

I'm sorry if individuals at your company or school are currently preventing you from using mobile devices at work. It's not their fault. It's just how they have been conditioned to perform. IT people are naturally a risk-averse group. They are expected to protect the company's intellectual property when it is on their network and devices. This is a good thing. Generally speaking, it just so happens that they have not been so good at adapting quickly.

Make no mistake: the market is changing rapidly these days. I knew some people that worked for a company that banned USB thumb drives. Not only did they do this, but the company also glued the USB ports closed to make them inoperable. Sure, this prevented people from copying files via *sneakernet* from one computer to another, but there were a number of holes in the theory. Use of FTP and a couple other common file transfer protocols on their network is still possible – granted some of these were a bit more geeky than the average user's skill level – so while these policies supposedly kept honest people honest, they did nothing to prevent the company from harm caused by people who really would have intended to do damage.

Many anti-social media policies in place at companies are much the same right now. Sure, you can't access Twitter, Facebook or YouTube at your desk, but you can via your 4G LTE smartphone or tablet. You can go outside for a social media break instead of a smoke break (it's healthier). You can't access company resources via your mobile device directly, but you can connect via VPN using some trial and error and have wholesale access to everything on your Droid. You see, these technology policies are often a joke. Most anyone who wants to circumvent the rules can likely do so. It's only a matter of time before the technologists at a company will relent. Provide a useful business case to management and stop bellyaching, and you might be able to help bring down that iron curtain of IT.

In 2010, Apple rejected or otherwise held apps hostage in the review phase because they were not using native Objective-C application code to produce them. I myself had an application in purgatory for nearly six months as a result. This dam has since been cleared, and the applications built using cross platform tools such as PhoneGap, Appcelerator's Titanium tool and others are indeed getting accepted into the App Store. To verify this, visit any of these companies' websites and look at the galleries they contain, then download and review the applications yourself. Dozens and dozens of such applications coexist peacefully in these markets alongside native applications. The general user populace won't notice any difference. As long as you don't run afoul of some basic premises that Apple has laid out, you will be fine. These rules apply universally to all applications. The rejections have a lot less to do with the actual tooling than they do with the disregard to some basic best practices, memory management issues, and perhaps even some usability problems.

Flurry estimated in August 2011 that worldwide, more than 600,000 apps were available for over 350 million iOS and Android devices. Consumers, according to Flurry, have downloaded over 65 apps per device (Newark-French, 2011). Your users are smart enough to install and use apps. Why can't a couple be your designs? It makes sense to me.

Now, what about the less-featured devices owned by many users (sometimes called *feature phones* as opposed to *smartphones*)? Accurately picturing the situation is a function of both surveying or knowing your audience, and understanding cell phone replacement cycles. You can target these devices using basic mobile Web design and even some app development tools. In the past, technology professionals commonly anchored their strategy by requiring full and equal support for the least-capable machines in their network and using a lengthy replacement cycle. With mobile, these cycles are shorter, and the technology landscape is far more consumer driven than the previous approach to technology strategy. Remember that you are not creating a strategy for right now, but for one to two years from now. Do you really want the low end of your audience to drive strategy or the enterprise, or do you want to get out in front of them and drive this boat yourself?

I thought so.

GOVERNANCE AND MAINTENANCE OF CONTENT

By now, you have some insight into the creation of content as well as its distribution. After it's out there in the hands of your learners, what then? After all, you haven't passed out dead trees. You haven't shipped CD-ROMs or DVDs to people. You don't have a fulfillment warehouse (or supply closet) full of binders and laminated job aids.

Matters such as lead time needed for replication or printing and drop ships become somewhat irrelevant when you have a virtual inventory. Mobile changes this. The governance and logistics of your content are now completely digital. There are no requisition forms to fill out. Little training for the trainer is required. New content changes in your websites and apps can be published immediately, keeping your instructional content in sync with your product information. Nearly as easy is the ability to keep your application code up to date as programming languages and operating systems are updated. In the mobile world, this sort of activity takes place at least annually, but can occur more often than this. You may need to monitor your developer centers at least monthly to check for new advancements in the software development kits (SDKs) you use to expand your mobile learning. Remember, this world moves quickly. The ease of republishing can seem a bit chaotic if you are not careful in laying some ground rules. Do not fall prey to this. Opening this can of worms can make it difficult to put the lid back on. You are going to need a roadmap to guide you.

While the title *czar* may be a bit draconian and cliché, in some ways you need someone with the authority to maintain and implement the roadmap when changes to the content strategy occur. Landmarks in this roadmap should be:

- Platform reassessments (for example, when do new OSs become a factor in your designs?);

- Content edits (likely synced with your product catalog updates);

- Device testing (someone is going to have get the new toys when they come out);

- Developer portal and account management (who submits apps, checks the stats, etc.);

- Device provisioning schedules (tracking UDIDs is no fun, but someone has to do it); and

- Interaction and co-planning with external stakeholder technology groups (IT, EIS, IS, GIS, whatever your company calls it).

Why are these important, you ask? For starters, platforms continue to evolve and disappear. What is a major market force today may not be tomorrow. Take a look at this graphic that shows the shift in the marketplace even since 2009 (based on aggregated data from comScore):

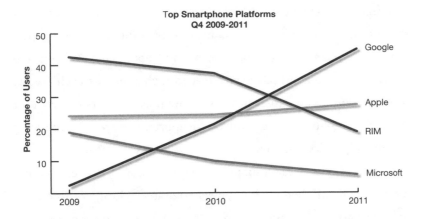

The market is constantly growing and changing, and constantly you will have to reassess your overall delivery strategy. At some points, apps may make sense for the process. Perhaps six months later, they won't. You'll need to pay attention to industry trends, but also to your workplace. What devices are making inroads in your company? Is IT planning an organizational buy of a specific new handset when it comes out?

Long-term content maintenance can actually be re-thought with this new distribution mechanism as well. Without CD/DVD printing or replication costs and no need to coordinate with the team managing the LMS, your Web-connected mobile learning can receive updates as the content changes, rather than having to wait for quarterly updates or shipping windows. It's pretty easy to make a mobile app that reaches out to a Web service from time to time and pulls down the latest content for local storage. This sort of semi-connected user experience offered by mobile learning is one of its greatest unsung benefits – an experience that you can take with you no matter where you are, and it remains in sync when you have an active network connection. You then have an augmented workforce even in remote locations, one that stays up-to-date when users leave and come back into range once again. Use this to your advantage. You can also think about your Web and app releases in staged approaches. Post just enough content to achieve the base function needed, then add new content as the users request it or as your organization's needs evolve – an approach known as producing a minimally viable product.

If your LCMS or LMS supports Web services as a delivery mechanism for content, then use it to power your apps. Don't let this cause a hold-up, though. It's easy enough for most Web design teams to set up a simple Web-based content management system these days, so maybe you can look outside your typical deployment options to make overall governance a bit easier in the long run.

Device testing can be a headache. While emulators or simulators are often good enough to provide basic compatibility, there is no substitute for real device-based testing. This can be done in the style of ad hoc team contribution, where the surveying you undertook previously is used to log the platforms, OSs, devices, and carriers you have available among team members and coworkers so that you can use these devices for testing as needed. I have a spreadsheet, for example, that lists some of my common contacts and the devices they currently possess, including any legacy devices. I swear I'm not a stalker.

You can take this one step further and request that people provide older or unused devices to your team for testing. It's a good opportunity to trade gift cards for what you may want. Another way to stay on top of this is to keep an eye on eBay, Craigslist, the classifieds and various grey-market mobile sites. Often you can get out-of-contract devices for a significantly reduced fee. Currently, in our test bed at my workplace, we have nearly two dozen such devices of various makes, models and operating systems – all amassed over some time, of course. Some were purchased new and unsubsidized – this is the most expensive way to build a collection because often these types of smartphones are $500 or more a piece – but most were either given to the team or bought used and out of contract. Some amount of creativity may be needed on your part to make this happen, but without a decent test bed, you will always have difficulty replicating fringe issues.

If you are in charge of the development team for you mobile efforts, you will have an important job because there are some responsibilities that only you can take, such as code signing and other sorts of governance topics. Without careful monitoring, you risk holding up team members from creating, distributing, and assessing various test builds. This world can be daunting. Distributed team dashboards, so common in today's software development world, are new to your average learning and development department. Most of these systems have good internal documentation, but to become familiar with them, you will need to do some heavy lifting in terms of research.

There is usually a hierarchical permissions setup in mobile software development Web portals. One person usually acts as the administrator. Under that individual, there are varying roles for developers who can build software and agents who can do administrative tasks like review analytics data, upload new versions of apps and complete other associated tasks. Many of these duties ultimately require approval from the team admin, so you'll need to be mindful of whom your team has put in charge when signing up for these roles with mobile software platform vendors such as Apple or Google. If you cannot be counted on to be available to approve workflows or sign certificates for developers, then you should likely delegate that role to someone who can.

In organizations where continuity of business is important, you may want to use email aliases for your team admins. An email alias is an email address that forwards messages sent to a substitute address of your choosing – i.e. sending a message to apps@yourcompany.com will send copies of the message to everyone listed as an alias recipient for that address. This way, if someone leaves a role at work, you can redirect the email alias on your end rather than negotiate with the developer portal owners or programs.

Depending on the platform – Apple, Blackberry, Android, etc. – there may be requirements for you or your developers to know a device's serial numbers or other unique identifiers in order to deploy your test builds on actual hardware. Apple, for example, uses an identifier called the UDID – or unique device identifier – that must be entered into a provisioning profile in order to allow a beta build to be installed. Managing devices can be a chore. It's best to assign a single point of contact to manage these devices, because there can be a finite number of them that you can add to these portals. Once you have exhausted your slots, you cannot add additional equipment to your testing profiles without some amount of trouble. Even if your development SDK doesn't require you to log or verify the device's identifier, be it serial number, IMEI, or otherwise, you can often use this technique on your own to verify that the application is only used on a device that is authorized. This can prevent unwanted users from causing potential security issues during the development and testing phases.

Other groups in your organization are probably investigating mobile options or have their own programs in flight. Asking around about what policies are taking shapes would be best for you, and while you're at it, see if there is an opportunity for your team to contribute to the discussion. Some services like security, reusable code frameworks, ongoing deployment, analytics and other administrative topics should be a shared responsibility across a number of departments. If you don't at least check with your counterparts in other areas of your organization to verify how issues are being handled there, you run the risk of doing a lot of legwork and wasting a significant amount of time and resources on a duplicated effort. Additionally, from a political standpoint you risk alienation by doing something out of step with the others and needing to redo everything. If your group hasn't been typically invited to the table in discussions like this, now is a good time to get in there. Mobile is shaping business today, and there are few organizations with enough expertise in this area to create great cohesive strategies. You may be an expert in your company and not even know it. By having an interest in this area, you have shown initiative and the basic requirement to enter into talks like this – the desire to get something done.

Quite the roadmap, right? With some forethought and adherence to a set of rules like this one, you are putting your team in the driver's seat of an important vehicle for business and productivity growth: mobile. You must remember that these policies should be strong and well-thought-out but also flexible enough to adapt to a changing marketplace. Technology always advances faster than bureaucracy.

IN SUMMARY

Content strategy may be a new concept to those in the learning field. It's been a vital part of modern Web content management for some time now. As we move to just-in-time information delivery, we should employ some of these techniques in order to maintain a roadmap for content.

We need to consider the creation of this content, or the how, why and what of the product to be crafted. You will begin to recognize that shrinking the courses to fit the small screen is not adequate for creating a great learning experience.

We also need a plan for the distribution of content. How will we get this information to our learners? Will we use an LMS or a Web content management system? Does this really need to be an app, or will a mobile Web or even an SMS experience suffice?

After the content is produced, who owns, publishes and maintains it? Who will ensure that the latest devices are compatible and keep our development and testing environments current? This represents a great opportunity to involve yourself with the technology department at your organization. Come with an open mind and fresh ideas.

FOUR

DETERMINING THE RIGHT PATH FOR YOUR ORGANIZATION

LINING UP NEEDS WITH EXISTING CONTENT

So we have a vision of what needs to be in our content strategy.

When you're first jumping to mobile, it's an excellent time to perform a soft reset of your training organization. That is to say, don't halt what you are doing, but take a step back, observe, analyze, report and review with your team the activities, assets and learning content you see. What have you been producing? Which elements have been the most successful? Where was there waste? For our purposes, waste means overtraining, missed messaging, unused assets, or produced materials that were overly complex or costly. Where did you not meet the learner's goals? Where are there gaps in the training that could be augmented with just-in-time delivery of information?

Conversely, where did everything go right? Which types of projects had the maximum effect on your learners' behavior and affected business results? Which products were well-received or got mentions in your organization's internal memos and newsletters? Did any of these ever elicit an excited hallway conversation or a kind word over a cup of coffee to let you know your team is on the right track? Sometimes the best ways to measure success can be a bit softer than an LMS report printout. Don't leave out the human side of feedback.

Once you have finished this assessment, you will likely see some trends. It could be that in your company, there is a certain type (or types) of training content or delivery method that works best for your learning audience. Perhaps it is instructor-led training for basics, coupled with eLearning for assessments and refreshing, then a job aid or similar performance support asset for on-the-job use. Maybe your company works best using a more comprehensive Web-based training curriculum and has done away with most classroom instruction. Perhaps you have some dyed-in-the-wool trainers that can facilitate successful workshops in their sleep, getting great results from your learners in the process. Whatever the outcome of your surveying, it's probably clear that certain roles, tasks or outcomes may not be working. These may be the best places to start when contemplating the content you want to use when you go mobile.

It's difficult to recommend diving in headfirst at this point. There are still some pieces missing from the puzzle. We must understand the scale and depth of what we are undertaking rather than just idly creating. Some forms of content are easier to transform than others. Some areas of your curriculum may have a dearth of assets or source content to curate or use for building something new. We aren't trying to enter into a situation that is going to require a massive rework, after all. We need to find information that is well formed, has a decent amount of positive reaction from the learners, and can be adapted to a content delivery format that jives with the technology profile and organizational culture. Anything less than that may set you up for a higher rate of failure. A first spin around the mobile learning track should be a good test for the migration plan, not a trial by fire.

All your needs, content availability, skills and resources must align in order to execute this first foray into mobile. You'll have plenty of opportunities to expand this later. First, we are looking for a great proof of concept, prototype, or small pilot that allows your management to make an informed decision about the value of mobile to your learners.

FINDING THE LOW-HANGING FRUIT

Ahh, the low-hanging fruit! Every organization has this – hence the cliché, right? This is the readily available, easily malleable kind of content that many people see, use or interact with. This might be an on-boarding module or a common job aid that is used by a wide swath of employees. If it's not too deep and has a well-defined set of learning objectives (no more than three to five), this could represent an opportunity to try it out in a mobile format. Brevity and focus matter here. These types of content might just be your low-hanging fruit.

Why are these examples great candidates for going mobile with your first efforts? Well, keep in mind these specific examples were only just that – examples. Your organization's low-hanging fruit might be a safety or compliance course, or a simple process diagram that serves as a reminder to everyone of how to perform a vital operational task that is easily forgotten, hence the need for a diagram. Whatever the factors pushing these pieces of content to the front of the list, listen to them here. More often than not, your gut reaction is going to be correct. After all, who knows more about how your content is being used and received than you?

When we go mobile, we are looking for a quick win – something the whole department, and eventually the organization, can get behind and use to recognize the value in moving to the new medium. We aren't looking for a lengthy project or anything that requires an overly rigorous analysis. Once you have the basics of your content strategy together, you want to move quickly and get something assembled that achieves the following initial goals:

• Can be completed without involving too many other departments;

• Can be built in a short amount of time;

• Is usable on a variety of devices that represents the general composition of your organization's technology landscape; and

• Provides a measurable result that you can take to management with a business case for doing more work.

This list of criteria is what really makes the low-hanging fruit. Even the most promising content will be hard to move to mobile if it fails on more than a couple of these points.

This early in the game, you don't want to involve too many outside people. You may draw far too much attention from individuals at other levels in the organization, and it's more likely to slow down progress than speed it up. For most jobs, any time you have to requisition resources or request assistance you know you are in for a lengthy effort.

You will want to go from concept to deployment in days or weeks, not months. Anything larger than that and I would be loathe to call it low-hanging fruit. This is why you need content in good shape and why you want to use some sort of tooling or development software that is reasonably familiar to you. This may be Flash if you are targeting primarily Android devices, or perhaps your software outputs clean, semantic HTML5. In this case you will be in a good place for using your content on a variety of devices.

This last point may be key to proving the usefulness of mobile to your whole company. If you are producing content that will be difficult for more than a quarter of your users, are you really serving their needs or are you serving yours?

DETERMINING WHICH PATH OFFERS THE GREATEST ROI

Once you have a few options in mind, it's time to assess which one will have the biggest overall impact when implemented on a large scale. This basic approach to projecting the return on investment (ROI) can be helpful in crystallizing an otherwise difficult decision. ROI is typically applied to larger projects, but it can also be effective to focus development efforts going forward by measuring some basic ROI on pilot programs. With some extrapolation and forecasting, you can start to see just how valuable the effort will be to the entire company when applied to more learners.

While calculating true ROI will be difficult at this point, you can begin to make estimates that will assist in your choice of pilot or prototype project. Here are some guidelines on the basic calculation you can use to get through this (from Woodill and Udell, 2011).

From an accounting point of view, calculating the ROI of mobile learning is relatively simple. Place a monetary value on the gross

program benefits of implementing a mobile learning system, deduct all
known related costs – which together make the net program benefits –
then divide the total by the known related costs. Multiply the result by
100 to express ROI as a percentage.

$$ROI\,(\%) = \frac{\text{Net Program Benefits} \times 100}{\text{Program Costs}}$$

For example, if the ABC Company implements a mobile learning program that costs $50,000 and produces measurable benefits of
$500,000, we can easily calculate its ROI. The net program benefits
are $500,000 - $50,000 = $450,000. Therefore, ROI is 900 percent.

Here's how the calculation works:

$$ROI\,(\%) = \frac{\$450,000 \times 100}{\$50,000} = 900\%$$

In this example, for every dollar invested in a mobile learning
system, there is a net benefit of nine dollars after all costs are covered.
This figure is usually expressed as an annual benefit, even though there
may be many long-term benefits. It is expressed this way because with
traditional classroom-based training, the impact usually diminishes
year by year. However, with mobile learning systems making information available on demand from any location, training can be reinforced
at any time, so this assumption can be challenged. We suggest that

benefits be calculated for the life of the project, as long as training can be renewed at any time the employee chooses.

The key to calculating ROI is listing all costs and benefits in financial terms – not an easy task! Not all cost and benefit information can be expressed as numbers; there are often intangible benefits that cannot be easily measured, making it that much more complicated to determine whether there was been positive ROI. Moreover, a focus on numbers tends to place an emphasis on the solution's efficiency, rather than its effectiveness. According to Craig Taylor (2002), "the learning profession has done a poor job of building core competence in quantifying the financial value and impact of most performance-improvement efforts."

Evaluating the return on training efforts is not just a matter of dollars and cents. The positive benefits of learning technologies such as mobile devices include increased speed of training to improve a new product's time to market, improved sales and commissions, increased safety on the job, and the ability to train hard-to-reach employees. It is not just a matter of saving money, although that is important as well.

Extending the benefits of mobile learning means recognizing that its specific *affordances* – what it does uniquely – can lead to innovation in and new approaches to training. Sometimes changing the approach to using a learning technology can turn a negative ROI into a positive one. For example, breaking learning content into small reusable learning objects (RLOs) has the potential to shift learning from a transmission model, in which an instructor dispenses information, to one in which where students find and help themselves to the pieces they need, when they need them. This ability can reduce instructor costs and increase the reuse of content, both of which have an impact on ROI.

In the initial strategy phase, any candidate program that's considered for piloting should have conducted some level of ROI planning. If your first work lands with a thud, it will be unlikely you will be granted funding for a second effort – much less a third – for some time. You probably won't get another chance until you can prove you have your bases covered in regards to the business, not just technology and content.

IN SUMMARY

Your organization has a unique set of content, resources and business needs. Understanding and cataloging these in the framework of your content strategy will allow you to identify your first efforts in the mobile realm. Use your organization's predilection for specific types of learning content to guide you while frankly assessing the state of your current content library. Sign up for an appropriate amount of work on your first efforts so that you can measure success and move on to the meatier issues you will soon face.

This is not enough. You must articulate the anticipated return on investment and plan for its measurement. Whether this is a true monetary return, increased productivity, reduced safety issues, or whatever you desire to measure, you will need to relay your plan to your stakeholders and measure your success on your stated objectives.

FIVE

KEY CONTENT TYPES FOR MOBILE LEARNING

MOBILE CONTENT: THE BIG PICTURE

Mobile learning is a large area unto itself. Just like eLearning, mLearning can be delivered in many different ways. eLearning delivery modes include traditional narrative and presentational learning delivery, scenario-based training, soft-skills training, games, and software simulation. Although mLearning is less mature than eLearning, it too can be delivered via differing modes.

I have identified the four primary categories of mobile learning, each with its own set of best practices and implied processes for creating, distributing and governing content (see next page):

Converted Content (e.g., eLearning, job aids, instructor-led training, performance support)

 Business Processes (SCM, ERP, CRM, contacts applications, custom-developed company software)

 Social and User-Generated (community-generated content, wikis, chat, Twitter, etc.)

 Uniquely Mobile (virtual or augmented reality, GPS data, other sensors, touch and haptics, voice and messaging services)

Those are some really cool categories! A few were probably expected, like moving eLearning to mobile, while others are perhaps a bit foreign to you. You might be asking yourself, "What is ERP?" The acronym stands for enterprise resource planning software, and it's used to manage large organizations' processes. Over the next few chapters, I will go in-depth discussing each of the four categories and provide examples for each that illustrate numerous technologies and design paths, show-ing just how broad a topic mLearning is.

The best part about these categories is that the instructional design model, the software tools, and the design and development processes for each one are independent of each other. We are only talking about the basic breakdowns of the content types for which we are planning to design, develop and deploy mobile learning. This means you can use the ADDIE approach if you want to. You can build the content in HTML, native code or use other rapid development tools that support mobile output. You can use agile development, or the waterfall method, or whatever you are most familiar with as your project management methodology. It's your call. Remember, these content strategies are less about the detailed designs for each type of deliverable and more about choosing the right conveyance for each piece of identified content in your learner audience's needs analysis, which you will have already completed. Certain needs lend themselves to specific content delivery categories. Constraints in technology or a learner's profile often dictate the actual designs used in the delivery strategy.

Sound a bit like mumbo jumbo at this point? That's okay. We'll get through this together! For now, just realize there is a recommended way to think about how your content can be repackaged, and there are levels of fidelity or interactivity in which you can then place this content to suit your users' needs. That ought to get you close enough for us to get down to business.

WHY BOTHER CATEGORIZING?

Mobile learning is a small change in thinking from what you may have previously considered training or learning. Mobile devices can be used for delivering eLearning-like content, reading books or watching long-form video. Witness the average device users in connectivity-constrained locations such as airplanes, sequestered coffee shops or away from WiFi networks that we now take for granted. Mobile devices are at their best when users are given free range and the ability to connect to services and cloud content. All the locations I just mentioned are closed settings. With their limited bandwidth and restricted contexts, they are a lot more like the classroom settings to which we've grown accustomed.

But mobile devices mean we need to rethink how we position content and job duties. People who use mobile devices have specific on-the-job needs that rarely align with traditional long-term learning scenarios. Instead they more frequently mirror the situations in which we use a cookbook, a dictionary, an encyclopedia or The Weather Channel. When we use these sources, we are most often looking for information that we can use to determine a new action plan to help us in an immediate situation. In his excellent book, *Tapworthy*, Josh Clark (2010, p. 32) outlines three primary use cases for someone using mobile devices:

- Bored – The user is looking to kill some time or otherwise occupy his- or herself;

- Local – The user is looking for specific information contextual to the situation at hand; and

- Microtasking – The user is interested in performing a specific task and only that task.

Clark then uses these cases to create a plan for application designers to produce either a utility app, an immersive experience or a reference app. While creating these artificial collections of user interface or user experience patterns does not seem necessary at first, it makes perfect sense when you consider how we interact with our devices in those specific cases. This heuristic knowledge was developed from the trials and failures of others and is vital at the outset in order to create a usable design and prevent developers from going astray from the application's original goals.

In mobile learning, we take these cases and layer the need to provide useful information – what is valuable in that context, at that time, to that person. For one, Clark's categories help us place a structure around how we talk about the work we are doing with others. Second, they help us define the people we need to work on projects. Third, the categories are helpful to our audience in the internal marketing and change management efforts that will accompany the work. Finally, the categories provide a tidy framework you can use in tandem with your larger mobile strategy – platform choice and procurement, device policy and provisioning, publishing and procedures – to help you realize exactly what to place on those shiny new devices.

Without a close look at this aspect, down the road you may just find yourself in a situation similar to this exchange:

Supervisor: Hey, can you get me a tablet version of those eLearning courses we just put on the LMS?

You: Hmm, not sure. Why do you ask?

Supervisor: Well, the VP just OK'd the purchase of 1,000 iPads to outfit the sales team while they're on the road. We need to have all courses ready to run by next quarter. Can't you just export them as HTML5?

You: Gulp.

Supervisor: Great, I'll touch base with you next week after you have a few of them done.

Take some time to research the best path to mobile and put a plan together, and the exchange could go a bit more like this:

Supervisor: Hey, can you get me a tablet version of those eLearning courses we just put on the LMS?

You: Hmm, it could be possible. Do you have any courses in mind? Who are the learners? Where will the courses be used? What device is it?

Supervisor: Well, the VP just OK'd the purchase of 1,000 iPads to outfit the sales team while they are on the road. We need to have all courses ready to run by next quarter. Can't you just export them as HTML5?

You: I don't think a straight conversion would be best. It could be costly and time-consuming and end up with mediocre, even bad results. I have some new ideas for what we could do that would leverage those mobile devices and breathe some life into our existing investment in instructional materials, though.

Supervisor: Hmm. Sounds interesting. What should we do to get the ball rolling?

You: Well, let me put together a brief covering some functional requirements and maybe we can draft a quick prototype for a piece of content or two.

Supervisor: Great, I'll touch base with you next week after you have that done. Thanks for the initiative!

One exchange gives you a headache and a lot of work to do. The other makes you an innovator and positions your team to drive the organization's direction as you go to mobile. It's obvious which situation I would rather face.

The four primary categories that I've outlined above provide a solid foundation for moving instructional content over to mobile. They enable you to propose productivity-enhancing applications and services with built-in learning to provide brand-new learning opportunities and to leverage your organization's thought leaders and best practices by using mobile devices' best built-in feature: communication.

Have I sold you on this yet? I hope so. Let's get down to it. How do we choose a category?

PICKING AND CHOOSING YOUR PATH

You are likely comfortable with the first category – content ported from other devices. Porting content over from your existing library may seem difficult, but it is doable. For many learning professionals, the other three are tougher to embrace. While many learning departments have moved into the social-learning realm by using tools such as wikis, blogs, Twitter, Yammer and SharePoint, there are just as many who are newbies in these applications. Take the next step and consider the other categories, such as using cameras and GPS, or perhaps integrating learning business applications like CRM, and at that point you will have probably left everyone else in the dust.

Learning professionals are often a risk-averse group. We like to take our changes in baby steps. ROI Methodology developer Jack Phillips has suggested that only 10-20 percent of programs reach Level 4 (impact) of his five-level evaluation framework, which also measures reaction and planned action, learning, application and implementation, as well as ROI (Phillips, 2012, p. 30). Additionally, Bersin & Associates analyst Karen O'Leonard wrote that in 2010, only 30 percent of companies spent money in informal learning (2011). The bottom line seems to be that few are able to formally measure the results from much of our work and there still remains a good many who are not trying out new or different avenues in the learning environment. This may be due to a lack of resources, or because we're fearful. Getting outside our comfort zones by jumping into brand new content types – non-porting content, building new services and learning products – may be a bit of stretch for those who are most comfortable facilitating a classroom or building an eLearning module.

Mobile is just that – it's mobile! Mobile learning is one of the new learning areas that are starting to turn heads. As time goes on and mobile devices become even more pervasive, mobile learning is likely to have an even greater transformative effect on training than eLearning did. With smartphones outselling other feature phones in 2011 (*2012 Mobile Future*, 2012, p. 10) and with nearly 12 million iPads sold during Apple's fiscal 2012 second quarter alone (*Apple Reports Second*, 2012), you can bet that a mobile learning tidal wave is already hitting us whether we are ready or not.

In choosing your path and identifying the categories of mobile learning you want to create, consider this: Choose your mLearning approaches and categories now, and drive that effort, or be prepared to have them drive you. Responding to the market is by no means a dishonorable act and when used well can provide great insight and success. However, as evidenced in the previous section, without some proactive learning, familiarity and experimentation, you may be steamrolled if you are not careful.

Responding fast enough to meet the demand for material can be difficult. Consider budgeting cycles, project timelines, SME availability, and now the precious commodity that is mobile developers, and you will be brewing the perfect storm of inability to meet your business partners' goals. You will also starve your learners of content they require, which is a risky position for you. If you are unable to serve their needs, you will find them going outside your trusted source to find their content in an app store or far worse – for custom development unbeknownst to the learning department all together.

So, what's my advice? For now your top priority should be to convert your best existing content to mobile in a usable, fresh user experience that's optimized for the devices used in your organization. Do this, and you can probably launch and succeed with something in this category in short order. It will take time and effort, and also courage. You can't hold yourself back because you're afraid to stub your toe. Success is worth the potential risk. Put a savvy, tech-friendly designer in touch with one of your most productive instructional designers (ISDs) and hit a home run.

Your next step should be to find the true social learning landscape in place at your organization. Whether or not you have deployed wikis and/or Yammer, your learners are already using social networking sites, likely on their phones. Trust me. Discover how they are already using these sites and see if there are ways to leverage or improve upon it. You should be aligning your mobile learning strategy efforts with any social learning enthusiasts on your L&D team and get working toward a common goal – a connected, helpful, collaborative workforce led by the top performers, sharing their tips with the rest of the organization in a meaningful, actionable way. A team member who is great at research and laying the groundwork for change management may be the one best suited for this task, as it could require some significant messaging.

The third step is to start looking down the unique avenues that mobile learning can take you. I'm talking about applications such as using GPS data to help your sales professionals with contextual information, or giving your technicians an augmented-reality view of the engine bay they are currently inspecting. How cool would it be to know exactly which bacterium was eating the plant in your learner's field? Sounds like the future, right? Not necessarily. Given current mobile technology, no performance-support applications that I've mentioned are outside the realm of possibility. Mobile devices are capable, pocketable computers that just happen to have a large array of great sensors and inputs. Using them to help your learners become more productive may just be the key to a nice productivity bump for your organization's business. The innovations in learning afforded by mobile devices offer the opportunity to see learning professionals as visionaries. I recommend putting a futurist or research specialist on this – along with an SME, if available – to start brainstorming. You may be surprised at what you come up with.

The last category to consider is line-of-business applications. It's probably the one with which you're the least familiar. When I first learned about line-of-business applications on mobile devices, I hadn't previously considered inline help, intelligent wizards, agents or contextual information in applications to be part of learning and development's domain. As our department's role shifts and as our organizations become fully mobilized, line-of-business applications may end up being a substantial portion of our instructional content.

Consider this scenario: The enterprise is about to launch a brand-new order-entry system that will be fully Web-based, an organizational first. There will be no desktop application, though there will be a Web-optimized version (with a mobile companion). Shortly afterward, a dedicated mobile app will follow, which will allow disconnected users to enter orders via their new iPads while on the road. You may have at one time built some software simulations, screen captures or screen casts and perhaps even written a text manual that was distributed via PDF. With one application target format – the desktop application – this was difficult enough. As the application grew or the scope changed in its development, the training had to change each time to remain accurate. That was bad enough with one version of an application. Now, multiply that by the number of browsers you will need to support, the number of mobile devices, then all the applications.

What you need to resolve this dilemma is less statically created help content and more contextual help pointers that can be applied to the fields and features in your application. Find an ally in your IT department, and divide and conquer. Get him or her to start an in-lining process for putting help content directly into the interfaces; then expand your thinking about how you'll train your users to use the software as it continues to evolve.

There you go – a bit of guidance on whom you might need to approach for the initial work on each content category, and how to do it. It sounds more difficult than it is. Dig in, and you'll get it in no time.

CATEGORIZING VS. CURATION

Once you have your content path(s) for implementing mobile learning in your organization, you may think there is nothing else to do with your content. It's tempting but not true.

Categorizing is not curation. These actions serve two different purposes in the design and development process. Categorization allows you to focus on the user's application usage in the equation. What will the experience look like? What will the primary functionality be? What data types or services will be available to the user, and how will access to those services work? The categorization you choose will reveal those bits of information to you as the design and development process unfolds.

Curation of content is choosing the best and most important content for your end users, which is different from categorization. Curating content to avoid overwhelming the user or creating a source that is difficult for them to use is vital. The metaphor of a live and unattended fire hose comes to mind. Without curation, something to limit the stream, there is too much information to handle, and the application becomes unwieldy and difficult for a user to control. A properly curated information footprint should not exceed the primary use cases planned in the application's design process. You can make related information or documents available through a progressive disclosure mechanism or perhaps in a *for more information* footer area, but you shouldn't feel compelled to make all the information in a subject area available on the front page. Really, you are setting out to publish the most useful information for a use case. This goal differs from providing an exhaustive resource or posting an ungroomed collection of content for your learners. Weeding out unneeded information is your duty.

You might consider the task of curation to be new, but it's not. You are probably curating content in your daily routine already. If you have ever read your morning news feed and selected one or two articles to tweet or email to coworkers, you are a curator, and if you also commented on why the information you sent them was valuable, you are providing an even more useful curatorial service, and you have a building block of mobile learning in there to boot – context. See? It's not that hard.

In moving to mobile, you will need to hone those curator skills. A simple, easy-to-use application or website which makes the most useful information available to users, with options to find more via links to data outside the application, is far more useful on the whole than a giant uncurated pile of facts and figures.

Curating information will become a vital job skill for you as an instructional designer as you begin integrating social and informal learning into your workforce training. With these additions, there will be large volumes of information coming at you. You will need to apply a curatorial hand to the content as it is created, along with signposts for its uses so that the learners know about the most valuable content, and so that misleading, inaccurate or outdated information is removed. Allowing everything to come through the feed – much like how an RSS reader or Google News works – will not provide added value to learners. You must act as the guiding hand.

Imagine, for a moment, a large content repository with a mobile template applied to the front-end design. This is an improvement over a desktop portal design where you need to pinch and zoom to even read the content, but you can do much better.

Why not use analytics and user surveys beforehand to provide short-cuts to frequently accessed pages and documents for mobile users? How about suggestions on those deeper pages to give the learner some avenues to pursue as needed? We are looking to balance information disclosure with ease of use and usefulness.

This effort may be an exercise that requires some trial and error to get right. I recommend capturing user feedback and usage data in any project where you think there could be need to adjust content depth or fine-tune your curatorial process.

IN SUMMARY

There are a lot of options for you in the mobile content development realm. It's important to recognize these and understand the different benefits they offer. The four primary types are:

• Content ported from other sources;

• Business process data ported to mobile and blended with training content;

- Peer-based or social learning; and

- Learning content made accessible via the unique affordances of mobile devices.

Knowing these types of content and understanding what each one offers will help you make the appropriate choice in going mobile. You must choose the path you need.

The four types of content offer a great framework for organization, but they shouldn't be viewed as a replacement for curation. You cannot dump a mass of content into a better-defined bucket. You will still need to practice restraint and carefully consider the appropriate detail level and information architecture in order to create a superior experience for your users.

SIX

CONTENT TYPE #1 DETAIL – REPURPOSING EXISTING LEARNING CONTENT

LEVERAGING YOUR LIBRARY OF CONTENT

How many courses do you have in your LMS? How many PDF hand-outs or PowerPoint presentations reside in the SharePoint server you use for instructor-led training? How about documents or images that you print as job aids? Likely, your count is in the dozens – if not hundreds – of discrete elements, right?

Does adding mobile learning to your delivery methods mean you toss those documents, pull down that LMS or stop improving your classroom materials? Of course not! That said, taking them directly into a mobile environment with no adaptations will not be your best bet either.

The quick answer is while it's a great idea to think that we can just move this content immediately to mobile, even in a readable format such as Word, Excel, PDF or a Web page, porting it over is probably not the best way to deliver content in a mobile format. Why?

One might argue that the screen is simply too small or the buttons are difficult to use. A myriad of other user interface (UI) and user experience (UX) issues may arise depending on the source material. The conduit through which we are delivering this content – a mobile device – is so powerful and so transformative in society that the fact we have repackaged our existing content and tossed it on the device may be of little interest to end users. When you have superlative mobile experiences available for little or no money downloaded billions of times, do you really want to take a chance that people might say that your work is only all right?

In your mobile phone, you have the power of a tremendous little pocket computer to leverage. Don't seek the easy button. Reinvent your content for when you push it onto the device. Anything less is doomed to the dustbin of dead apps and pixels. What we are looking to do when we go mobile with our content library is more like a mix tape of modern mash-up recordings, not just a remastered boxed set of training.

How do we begin? Let's look at the most popular forms of content used in most learning curricula. We'll go through each one in more detail later:

- Instructor-led material/Classroom training;

- eLearning, a.k.a. WBT or Web-based training, CBT or computer-based training;

- Documents and data;

- Performance support;

- Just-in-time bulletins; and

- To-do lists, checklists and inspections.

You may have types other than those listed above, depending on your industry. If you do, then analyze these additional documents and line up each of them with one of the above. It's nearly impossible to think of all the various types of instructional materials used across numerous design models and development processes.

INSTRUCTOR-LED, ELEARNING AND BLENDED MATERIAL

Just as there was a rush in the early 2000s to move *all* instructor-led training to an eLearning delivery mechanism, we are beginning to see the same scenario play out in the mobile space. I hope I don't need to tell you why this might not be a great idea, but I'm sure you recall how we stubbed our toes doing this the first time. Simply put, not every piece of instruction can be completely divorced from its original delivery format and just plopped into a new system, nor should it be.

When moving instructor-led training to a Web-based delivery format, there were instructional design and technology differences, as well as graphic and media design changes that needed to take place. Since instructor-led training offers opportunities for discussion as the materials are covered, and the presenter his or herself can adapt messaging as needed to handle the learners' needs, slides or presentations can vary greatly from session to session, and each learner can take away a personalized experience. For the most part, eLearning does not offer this flexibility. As an employee, you are usually taking the same courses as your colleagues.

The possibility of personalization means that converting instructor-led materials mobile may be a better fit than moving them to eLearning. The best mobile learning is usually just in time, just the right amount, and just for the user. There are parallels between the way a user will move through mobile lessons and the way the instructor leads you through content point by point and responds to your inquiries with his or her personal touch. Mobile learning is delivered at the point of need and used as a reference rather than a base of knowledge. There is still opportunity for an instructional designer to allow room for self-direction, exploration, and a progressive reveal of deeper knowledge upon request while your mobile learning module, app or website is in use. This can mirror the baseline of data given during classroom learning, wherein learners are interested in getting more information, having a discussion or hearing a counterpoint based on what has just been relayed to them.

Personalization is more effective for many learners when you consider how a few choose to interact or not interact in a classroom setting, especially when they are unsure of themselves or how the rest of the class may react. I'm sure we have all been in a setting where we have wanted to ask a question but hesitated because we weren't sure if it was the right time or if we would sound unintelligent or incompetent. With the personal and private nature of mobile learning, these fears can be assuaged. Because my use of mobile learning is truly between myself and the content, and because my ability to dig deeper into the content does not hamper or alert other learners, it can be a process of self-discovery that will not derail training for others.

Here are a few crucial points to keep in mind as you consider moving instructor-led, eLearning or blended training to mobile:

- Traditional training is, in most cases, information that is given ahead-of-time, and it often contains more detail than may truly be needed to do the task for which a learner is being trained. Distill your mobile messaging to the bare essentials for most users.

- Instructor-led, eLearning or blended training is usually given in a mentor/mentee or teacher/learner dynamic. This is removed when the delivery is changed. In mobile learning you must provide an easy-to-use interface and reassure the learner that the content is authoritative, or you may lose that from-the-expert feeling that is so vital in making learners realize that the content is important.

- Consider housing instructor-led content in more explore-able information architecture. A branching, highly browsable interface arranged by topic or task may be a great option here.

- Provide a search or query function so that learners can interact with the system and retrieve the results they want to see. Because this will be used at or around the point of need, we want to make sure that we are not forcing learners through a progression of content that harkens back to a day of courseware. The content should instead serve as an augmentation to information they already have in their possession or have received at some point.

- Instructor-led classes, eLearning and other traditional educational materials are meant to be consumed in traditional learning environments. These environments are devoid of distractions, context and other real-world diversions that often make delivering a full course difficult or impossible.

- Learning materials like these are usually at least 30-45 minutes in length but can often be over 60 minutes in duration. This depth is overkill for most mLearning and will probably act against you in most cases. Let's not forget that smartphone users tend interact with their devices anywhere from about 10 seconds to about four minutes (Falaki et al., 2010, p. 4). Do what you can to make your information digestible in that format.

- These devices have a far smaller disk capacity and computer memory (RAM) allotment than what a laptop or desktop has. We must optimize our media because of this and use guidelines from the device manufacturer to determine the appropriate media encoding and file size for selected delivery formats.

- The user interface for mobile must be more concise and straightforward than anything you may be building for your eLearning. In eLearning we can get caught up in building more complex layouts and menu structures in the pursuit of engagement. This leads to disuse and app deletion in the mobile world. Do not fall prey to the cool overdose that so many of us did in the eLearning world. If the app's navigation must be learned to use the app at all, then it's a failure.

- Simplify, simplify, simplify.

Let's take a look at several basic approaches to eLearning and how they can transition to mLearning. Here is a wireframe of an eLearning course used to help onboarding. This screen in particular is a timeline representing the history of the company, showing its rich 100-year history.

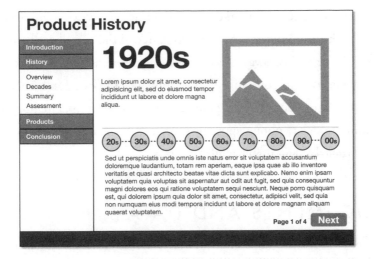

Contrast that with an adaptation of that content for use in an mLearning implementation. Note the reduced overall interface footprint and the mobile-friendly approach to scrolling through milestones in the company's history.

The differences are marked and intentional. We've significantly reduced the user interface chrome and flattened the overall course hierarchy. We've tucked away the course navigation and made it familiar to anyone used to common mobile apps like the one for Facebook, and we've introduced natural gesture controls used for pagination and scrolling in smart phone apps. In short order we've made the course more navigable and usable while on the go.

DOCUMENTS AND DATA

We all have them – the content libraries. Most of us have them piled away in SharePoint servers and other document repositories, but make no mistake: they are there. Often neglected, sometimes berated, these nooks and crannies of information contain a number of gems. After all, they were created in order to provide a single source or safe haven for valuable content for the enterprise, right?

Why do these document sources so often fall into disuse over time? The answer lies in the user experience that these warehouses deliver. At most times, these sources are uncurated and offer little information that can guide the user.

As a mobile learning resource, unfettered access to such a wealth of information might seem like it was heaven-sent. After all, wasn't it just yesterday that we remarked how great it would be if we could retrieve these resources no matter where we were? Let's not fool ourselves here. Unrestricted, unassisted, uncurated access to information rarely results in productive user interaction or a positive user experience. In fact, loosely arranged content in an interface that is tough to browse or search, coupled with limited or reduced connectivity, content consumption capabilities, and smaller screen sizes seems like a recipe for disaster.

There are various ways to better your content delivery, though.

- If you are using older document repository software, and you have been considering upgrading, now is the time to investigate your options. Is the newer version of your software mobile-friendly? How do you know? Can the vendor provide you a best-case example of the software in a mobile-friendly format? How about an out-of-the-box experience? These can often be worlds apart from each other. I have seen far too many implementations fall short due to a lack of resources at rollout to create mobile-friendly templates and UIs.

- Hone your UI to match your target platforms. Users of touch-screen smart phones are different from users of non-touch-screen phones. Tablet users are a whole different class as well. Without carefully tuned UIs for each of these audiences, you risk alienating each in different ways.

- Personalization of the user experience is an important consideration. Allow the user to pin, bookmark or marks items as favorites. Use metrics and analytics that help page templates provide quick access to frequently-accessed data. A recommendation engine like Amazon was seemingly an unreachable goal for many people just a few years ago, but many platforms are starting to integrate this feature into their application programming interfaces (APIs).

- Social features should not be excluded. Use content ratings, reviews, and comments to provide more meaningful context around your content. Give your users signposts and search-friendly way-finding to help them use their queries to produce meaningful results.

- Encode your media to be more mobile friendly. You cannot continue to say, "Well, our video use on mobile is really small right now. I just cannot justify encoding or moving over our content at this time." This becomes a self-fulfilling prophecy. It's not difficult to re-encode a few videos to the mobile-friendly H.264 standard and track the change in usage that results. You may be surprised at the uptake.

- Whenever possible, make document content available and searchable without extra application installs or downloads. Your goal is to reduce barriers to entry, not make more of them. The closer you can get the document into a user's tablet or smart phone, the better.

Take a look at the typical document repository interface for a non-mobile-optimized template:

When you contrast that with the simplified, easy-to-use, user-centric and mobile-optimized design below, the choice is pretty obvious as to which you would prefer when you are on the go.

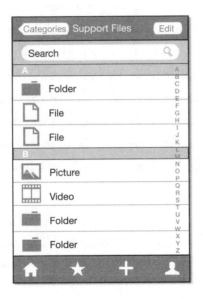

I've emphasized search and smarter browsing methods. I've also introduced the concept of bookmarked or favorites. While the term in your system might be *recommended for you* or *common files*, the basic concept is the same. These features provide quick access to content that a user either needs to see or uses frequently.

Office and productivity software are a big part of your average knowledge worker's learning workflow. Make the software available and easy-to-use, either as a Web app or dedicated mobile application, and your old document repository may gain a new lease on life.

PERFORMANCE SUPPORT

Performance support software – sometimes called an *electronic performance support system* or EPSS – is a vital part of many workers' lives today. The average set of jobs that people are expected to perform is so complex that requiring people to have everything they need to know memorized or as a psychomotor skill would be impossible. Most people need reminders or help to complete more complex or less frequently required tasks. EPSS first came to the attention of the learning and organizational performance community in the early 1990s, and there are many definitions of what it really is. Gloria Gery is most often credited for creating the term and wrote a book about it in 1991. The shorter definition in Barry Raybould's 1995 paper is one of my favorites:

> An EPSS is the electronic infrastructure that captures, stores and distributes individual and corporate knowledge assets throughout an organization to enable individuals to achieve required levels of performance in the fastest possible time and with a minimum of support from other people.

Good performance support materials are easy to use and available at any time, and they help employees in the context of their work. For these reasons, mobile is a perfect choice to help your workers do more while on the job. Mobile devices are meant for easy use and are almost always carried by a person. Mobile devices are available in a learner's context and often can ascertain a user's context via sensors and other onboard features.

Good performance support materials are so simple to use and so invaluable that people would be foolish not to have them in their toolkits when they leave the office, enter the worksite, or go on the road.

What's great about mobile is that with 90 percent of us carrying a mobile device, we can have the technology and ability to access just-in-time information that will help us make knowledgeable decisions from anywhere.

Much has been written on the effectiveness and core functions of performance support, with industry leaders like Bob Mosher leading the way and offering cogent advice on this topic. "Real learning happens as we work," Mosher says, "Research shows that 80 percent of learning in the workplace occurs on the job, rather than in formal training sessions" (*New Book by Bob Mosher*, 2011). Performance support and just-in-time information are key elements of this type of learning. Mosher adds, "The purpose of training isn't just about disseminating knowledge and building mastery of it; it's also and more importantly about building competency to perform and enabling performance across changing contexts" (as cited in Allen, 2009). Those contexts are the times a learner is in process. Mosher's well-known "Five Moments of Need" is an industry standard and is valid regardless of the technology used to deliver just-in-time information.

As a refresher, Mosher's Five Moments of Need occur:

1. When learning for the first time;
2. When wanting to learn more;
3. When trying to remember and/or apply;
4. When something changes (even when the change is minor); and
5. When something goes wrong. (Gottfredson and Mosher, 2011).

We must remember our overall goal in performance support and not linger needlessly on the design or its basic development and delivery. A colleague of mine has a great anecdote about a successful performance-support effort that consisted of creating JPG images and sending them to people via email so they could store them in their image libraries. Talk about low-tech – there were no servers, apps or any analytic platforms required. The total investment was minimal, and the timeline for deployment was short.

Performance support systems, however, can become advanced. You can tie them to customer relationship management (CRM) systems, or perhaps use an LMS or other analytical platform to track the overall use and engagement that you are seeing, but you don't have to if you're just getting started or need a quick win. These tools should not be over-thought or complex in their execution. Sometimes the simplest answer is the best.

That said, if you have a great services-oriented architecture (SOA) in place for your technology platforms, then there is good reason to move away from simplicity in your performance support systems. When you create a just-in-time solution that ties into other systems like CRM, SCM or ERP, you know you can accomplish something amazing. Legacy systems can be tricky, but most major enterprise software packages developed in the last 3-5 years have some form of service or module in place that can be implemented to bring perfor-mance support functionality to the user. The same goes for LMSs. Many view the LMS as a walled garden that cannot be broken down. There are a growing number of LMSs out there, though, that enable data interchanges via XML, JSON and other formats. If you have great performance-support materials already in the LMS that would succeed on a mobile device – and your Web services layer permits this form of communication and data translation – then research what is required to publish that content in the easiest way possible. If this last bit of information seems interesting but maybe too technical, take the book to your resident geek and ask if your systems are capable of this.

Here are a few considerations to note in the user interface and user experience departments as you design your first performance-support tool. With many performance-support tools, such as job aids existing as printable PDFs, you will need to devote time to redesigning the content so to be easily read on the handhelds your workers will use in the field. Multi-column text, heavily ornate typefaces or non-standard, non-HTML fonts should be avoided. Consider the following job aid layout:

With a few hours of a designer's time, stripping out the unnecessary elements and reformatting the content to a single column using HTML and CSS, you can have an easy-to-read, navigable piece of performance support. See the revised version on the next page:

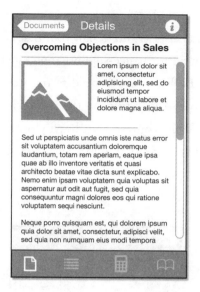

You can also use job aids to augment the user interface with a nice icon-driven menu system, or perhaps integrate zoom capabilities into didactic images and workflow depictions. The idea is to capitalize on the new-found capabilities these devices have made possible. There are many new tools in our kits that make the PDF seem downright antiquated when you think about all the great sensors and features these devices have and how we can bring them to our user to enrich the content, all the while increasing its ease of access and overall use.

I have had a number of heated discussions with learning professionals about performance support and its increasing importance in the training and learning professional's toolkit. I am all for people learning about the content ahead of time when the return on investment and a learner's ability to retain warrants it. There are lessons that should be learned in advance so that a professional can respond appropriately and not necessarily fall into a reactionary mode at the time of application. That can be perilous depending on your profession. Surgeons, pilots, skilled tradespersons, and all who work in hazardous or high-pressure environments cannot live on just-in-time learning alone, nor should they. That type of learning, though, excels in many other situations:

- Augmented simulation and coaching applications. Are there ways we can assist people with at-the-ready answers while they work?

- Workflow management and adaptation. How do you respond when the unthinkable occurs? Can our device interact with our settings or be aware of our situation and offer expert advice?

- On-the-fly or ad-hoc communication. Think of phoning a friend on *Who Wants to Be a Millionaire?* Don't forget that these devices have voice capabilities, too. If you aren't able to call a human, a robo-dial or SMS text messaging system could be an option.

- Diving deeper. The point of need is often a subtopic of a task. There are likely deeper or related tasks, though, where a user could also use a review. Can you use a system of metadata to expose related content to users as they are working in order to augment their further activities?

- Adaptive learning systems that leverage metacognition. When a learner can pinpoint his or her best way to learn, we often see huge gains in retention and learning. Are there content strategies that we can introduce that enhance this awakening? If we create performance support systems that push the discovery process further and faster, that seems like a great way to accelerate learning for our users.

My main recommendation when faced with skepticism is that the following be considered: Does your content teach learners to complete a task more safely and productively? Yes? Then why worry about the time and setting in which it is applied, or whether an assessment or other traditional hallmark is present? Sometimes contributing to the organization's bottom line is seen as a secondary goal for training, but isn't that what keeps us all gainfully employed?

JUST-IN-TIME BULLETINS

Product bulletins are changing. You no longer need to send documents for duplication or worry about the PR wire news cycle. With mobile devices in the hands of your audience, you have an always-connected group of learners ready to absorb your latest content.

The actual files could be PDFs or Word docs, and perhaps they could even use the same layout you are using for the print or Web versions. The notification and messaging for this content type is everything, though. If the information is truly mission-critical, you need to examine how you are sending your information to your learners. You may need to examine SMS or perhaps iMessage or BlackBerry Messenger (BBM) solutions in order to get your audience the freshest information in the easiest format for them. Other options include older techniques such as email updates or RSS. These still work and have a low-technology threshold to implement. A number of modern mobile app platforms support the use of push notifications. These may be a valid, user-preferred way to distribute updated information. Again, this all goes back to your need to understand your audience.

If your audience is under the impression that they will never need to bother with the content you push out unless it's of paramount importance, then you must be mindful of this. A high-price, high-profit tag industry obviously has differences in how the product or service is sold when compared to a low-price, low-margin item. Then again, depending on the seriousness of the information in the bulletin, you may need to consider how you can break these simple social contracts and relay the information in an appropriately serious manner.

TO-DO LISTS, CHECKLISTS AND INSPECTIONS

Ahh, the clipboard-inspection checklist! Somewhat nostalgic and hated at the same time, these little pieces of necessity have served a great purpose in safety inspections, preflight activities and so many other industries for decades. They enable us to make certain the task is done right. Many professionals wouldn't go out on the job site without these.

These helpful aids may be as simple as basic to-do lists scribbled on the backs of yesterday's tear-off calendars, or they could be software products that are part of a getting-it-done methodology. These more advanced systems are a rarity though. With the adaptation of mobile technology rapidly becoming *de riguer*, the age of the digital checklist is coming. I can't wait.

Consider for a moment a foreman's daily routine. He is responsible for the safety of his workers and the overall condition of the equipment and worksite, and his current inspection duties probably require the use of a checklist. This is likely a paper-and-pen affair with a carbon copy triplicate implementation. What if, just as a lark, this clipboard was replaced by a 3G tablet that had a digital version of that same checklist connected to a database, that logged the foreman's activity and stored the state of every piece of equipment, the workers, and the workstations in that worksite? This checklist could be far more than just a record keeper. It could be an active, dynamic document that empowered the manager to see the state of equipment and obtain information on a particular machine, such as its service records, or spot potential issues before they arise. Taking into account human safety issues, the checklist application would know that a machine's usual operator is currently out sick and would need to be staffed by a less-experienced person. Talk about just-in-time information! This is just one simple example from a single industry. What kinds of applications can you envision for digital checklists in yours?

Atul Gawande's excellent 2010 book, *The Checklist Manifesto*, offers an enlightening view on such a thought. What happens when industries introduce a checklist, performance-support-driven approach to ensuring safety and compliance with best practices? If checklists can help surgeons and airline pilots to better do their jobs with less error, why shouldn't you apply that mindset to your field? Are you an arborist securing a job site for the safe excision of a problematic tree? Do you have a checklist for that? What if you are an attorney about to file a civil suit against someone for not properly securing a job site, and your plaintiff has incurred damage? Do you have a check list for the paperwork? Did those who failed to secure the construction site use a checklist? All these are scenarios in which a checklist can help you. A set of digital checklists that can be recorded in a centralized database or cloud instance is even better. Think about the possibilities from a risk-management standpoint. Consider the amount of increased productivity you would see when people have instant support to prevent them from missing steps in their jobs. Brilliant!

Let's look at a couple of quick examples of checklist-like approaches to a mobile user interface design. Consider this multi-tiered list of checklists:

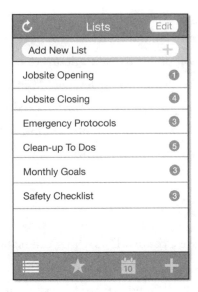

After drilling into the list, let's examine a user interface for the detailed view:

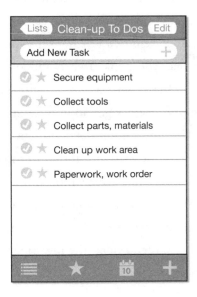

Checklist and getting-it-done approaches to performance support are the bread and butter of mobile learning. They are essentials – simple solutions to common problems. With tie-ins to back-end systems and processes, as well as the ability to leverage Web analytics and other measurement tools – perhaps even an LMS if needed – they just might be the easiest way to deploy measurable, successful mobile learning to your workforce. They should not be overlooked.

IN SUMMARY

It's possible you have a content library that can be brought over to the mobile world. It's important to understand that even though many of your existing files and modules can be read or at least opened, you shouldn't stop there when it comes to handheld devices and tablets.

It's vital to realize that the path to creating great mobile learning will require some rethinking of your content in order to maximize its effectiveness. We must examine the main text and instructional content, just as we did when we moved instructor-led training over to mobile, but information density and ease-of-use on these devices are far more important than you think. You should look at ways to minimize esoteric user interface conventions to which you may have grown accustomed and simplify the navigation in order to reduce barriers to entry for learners. Content redesign and the optimization of media assets will also need to be factored into the conversion process.

When providing just-in-time information to learners, consider the document repositories and intranet resources you may already have out there. Providing a mobile-optimized user interface to a SharePoint site or wiki may be a great way to extend the investment on your existing learning portals.

Performance support and product bulletins are a natural match for mobile learning. We want to make sure we are taking advantage of the new possibilities these devices offer us. We can easily move job aid documents over to smart phones and tablets, but perhaps there are easy-to-implement tweaks that will make these documents more attractive for use by our on-the-go learners.

Considering how many of us already use these devices as productivity tools, it's not surprising to think that a great way to increase your workers' outputs may be to offer a similar suite of tools in order to get them through their tasks.

With a bit of forethought, you can move learning content over to mobile from existing sources. This needs to be done with proper consideration and planning. It doesn't happen by pushing an easy button, but you can make it to the finish line with great success if you simplify your learning content and focus on the user's goals.

SEVEN

CONTENT TYPE #2 DETAIL – LINE OF BUSINESS AND PRODUCTIVITY

WHEN IS LEARNING NOT LEARNING?

For our second category of mobile learning content, we are boldly going where few learning departments have gone before: the line-of-business application. I'm talking about adding instructional content to mobile applications, produced by the organization for use by the employees to complete assigned tasks.

By relegating your content to the classroom, eLearning purgatory and job-aid realms, you are probably not doing enough to affect organizational performance. Based on a correlation between the content you produce and your learners' overall output, you are probably reaching a fraction of the total workforce you are supposed to assist in a real and meaningful way.

This may be due to a lack of direction in instructional design, an ever-shrinking budget, or even basic learner apathy. Regardless of the cause, mobile learning gives you an opportunity to fix this. To do so, you are going to do more with less.

You will claim more ground in the war for attention, produce more helpful content in the direct line of fire. You are going to get in your learners' faces in every mobile application from the organization. This will be done by developing less code, crafting fewer simulations, and printing less paper.

This content type has spurred the most energetic and passionate discussion in my travels, presentations, hallway conversations, and as a result of my Twitter rants. Many learning professionals believe that putting instructional materials in the apps that your coworkers use every day is not learning. Instead, they view it as a form of performance support or even worse – an IT task. I understand the trepidation. When three-letter acronyms (TLA) get tossed around in a room of learning professionals, these foreign terms usually earn a few blank stares. But think about this: If you could put an instructional designer's imprint on the most vital apps that people use every day – whether it is customer relationship management (CRM), supply chain management (SCM), enterprise resource planning (ERP), or any other systems you have in place that could be leveraged more effectively – why wouldn't you? Why wouldn't you want your team involved in the successful launch of a major mobile initiative, shaping how these next-generation services are crafted and rolled out?

Let's not get too hung up on the L in L&D for just a moment. Don't you have at your core a goal to improve your organization's bottom line? Aren't you there to help people achieve? Don't you get a budget to train people, with the ultimate goal being increased revenue? You don't have to let your inner academic die. You don't even need to stop thinking about curriculum development or your pedagogical approach to content. All I am asking you to do is to consider devoting a small amount of your team's total allocation to exploring this new area. Maybe you need to take a step back to reexamine your mission statement and vision for what you do. I'm sure it says something more akin to "improve our organization's productivity and performance" than to "build pre-event learning content." By turning your back on the usual avenues for extending your reach into the rest of the company's processes, you are expressing the opposite of your intended mission.

It is likely that you have built software training before. It may have been a screen-capture-based production with some pauses to ask the users to input data into fields or select checkboxes on a form before moving on to the next steps. Maybe it was a more in-depth simulation or perhaps a reproduction of the software itself, emulated in an interactive experience. How much time and effort did you spend creating this? Granted, a few rapid tools have made this type of training easier to produce, but it's still a cost center that would be great to reduce, right? What is somewhat crazy about this training is that often newer (especially Web-based) applications have built-in contextual help, yet vendors are still devoting countless hours to incremental updates in their training applications to help users better utilize the software. Why are we still providing so much ahead-of-time training for these systems when most issues that people will have with the software will be point of need or application problems?

Data entry, customer relationship management, business-process management, claims, accounting, support systems, and call-center applications – the list of business applications is nearly endless. Custom software built on Web services is pervasive in enterprises these days. The trend is pushing a lot of these to mobile via smartphone and tablet apps and mobile-optimized websites. Don't let the teams putting these projects out there get ahead of your learning and development group. Get in on the ground floor and make sure the user experience of these applications has support and learning in mind from the get-go. Your job as training gatekeeper and usability expert will be to ensure a simple, pleasurable user experience.

CRM AND OTHER BUSINESS PROCESS INTEGRATIONS

You log into a number of systems at work every day that have little to do with learning and are key line-of-business applications. These applications were probably built and deployed by the enterprise-systems group, not your department. This makes sense. After all your workgroup doesn't build enterprise software, does it? Due to time constraints and lack of skills required to do that kind of work, we would agree that we can't and don't want to get into that line of business. While this is true, there remains a distinct opportunity emerging with mobile technology and mobile learning.

As the systems group introduced desktop applications over the last few years, did your group help produce the training materials and inline contextual help? If so, great! If not, why not? You missed a direct line to the users of the software. These applications are used daily by many of your potential learners. You can choose to either put your educational content into the application, deploying it with the software itself, or develop training after the fact.

With mobile software's agile development methods and the rapid timelines for deploying these products, it is crucial that you respond more quickly than you ever have. If you wait too long to commence the training component of your project, your software may already be under revision, and a number of new mobile handsets may have been introduced for which you must build new content.

Currently most mobile platforms have relatively weak multitasking capabilities caused by processing power and constraints to display and input. Couple this with the need for speed, and your training problem becomes acute. You probably won't be able to produce training for the applications or services that are easy enough to access during regular workflow. Creating compelling instruction that will inspire the users to switch from the actual experience is also a challenge. For these reasons and to maximize reach and reduce wasted effort, I recommend that you partner with your application developers to create software with *integrated* training and educational content.

Consider the results when you put the following information directly into the tools that your professionals use:

- Training content is now available for use in the software itself. The user does not need to leave the system to learn how to use it.

- Tips and tricks for increasing productivity can be offered using the software and the processes that it manages.

- Soft-skills training or reminders that reinforce proper use of the software can be included.

- Contextual help on the trouble areas is possible for added performance support.

- Expert systems and other inline wizards can be added with appropriate copy and media resources written by instructional designers, not the developers.

Contrast these benefits with several of the common issues and waste we encounter when moving to another system:

- Duplicated training content – one set from the developers, one from the learning and development group. This is the epitome of waste in training content.

- Out-of-date content – after all, you need to wait until the application build is completed before any training content can be built. This automatically places you behind schedule even before your effort has started.

- Help and training content produced by non-training personnel – who knows the best methods to help your learners? A programmer or a professional paid to enhance productivity, who is tapped into the organization's strategy and understands the learner's goals? If your answer is the programmer, please do us all a favor – put the book down now and get some fresh air.

Let's take a look at a couple of interfaces for current sales tools, such as your CRM system. A typical desktop CRM user interface might look like this:

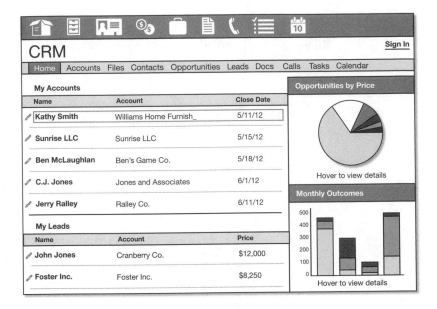

When you take this interface and redesign the bare minimum to move it to a mobile interface, what happens? Take a look:

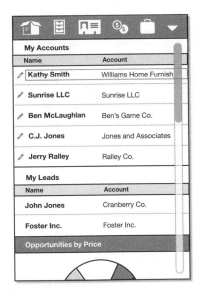

There are many of fields and inputs and no guide to help the user. Contrast that with a similar UI, but adjusted with just a few guides:

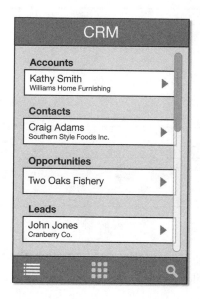

Let's try this on for size: A simple "?" button in the UI that aids the user by entering help mode. After tapping the question mark, any subsequent tap action brings up a dialog or overlay that helps the user by providing instructions, context, and perhaps accompanying instructional media such as images or videos in short order, all on demand.

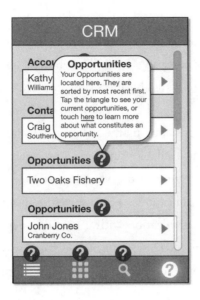

Now this is what I am talking about. The user interface help system is useful and unobtrusive. It lets users finish tasks and also seek help as needed.

This is mobile learning in the flow of the work, not systems-building or an IT task. This form of instruction is crucial to the number one job skill of any 21st-century knowledge worker: digital literacy. Improve your users' digital literacy, and see the results. Shun this type of work, and slowly see your influence and budgets chipped away by and delegated to the teams that will produce this content for the organization.

CUSTOM BESPOKE APPLICATIONS

"We want an app for that!" This is the rallying cry of every department of every organization of scale in the smart phone and marketing-driven culture we work in.

Stonewalling against this trend is a strategy that only works for so long. When this request comes from an executive or a group of top performers in your company, we will see how it quickly goes from a slogan in a commercial to a business case and RFP. I have seen dozens of such requests as a consultant. A few are valid and needed as enterprise proprietary apps, but many are served by either mobile Web development or even available commercial products.

The two latter categories aside, what do we do for custom-developed (a.k.a. "bespoke") applications? These solve the specific business needs of the sponsoring organization with a privately deployed application that is fully customized. These applications come with a price in terms of development as well as the cost of training the employees who will use the system.

Many custom applications launch with training as an afterthought, delivered after completion. Little consideration is given during the development phase to use the notes and business-case documentation to build either the test cases that would verify that the application met its goals or the documentation that would help the end user with day-to-day system interaction.

Inserting the training folks into the pipeline to assist with documentation is a big deal in many organizations. I know it will require striking partnerships with the development group and perhaps outside vendors. As mobile applications become an increasingly visible part of the enterprise's technology footprint, this is only going to become even more important.

Consider this: more than 85 percent of respondents to an ASTD/i4cp study "indicated their company provides mobile devices to at least some of the workforce, but less than 30 percent did so with tablet computers" (Lykins & Wentworth, 2011, p. 23). Couple this with

72 percent of companies who responded to an October 2011 *Good Technology* survey that formally supported a bring-your-own-device (BYOD) program for their employees. Another 19 percent "indicated they were either planning to support within the next 6-12 months or were considering but did not have a specific timeframe for support" (*Good Technology State*, 2011, p. 5). As I posited in previous sections, this could be the best opportunity for you to contribute directly to your organization's bottom line.

Take a look at a couple versions of a custom application. First, one with no instructional content or help in it:

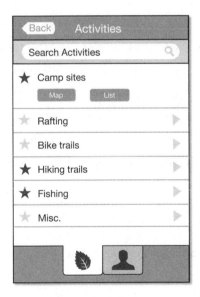

Next, with a few tweaks in the UI to help the user by way of instructional design:

If your company isn't already exploring this type of application development, just wait. Just as you saw a boom in custom VB script and battleship grey applications in the early 2000s, then a boom in RIA and AJAX applications in the latter 2000s, so too will you see a boom in custom mobile application development, all done by your in-house systems team(s). Get on board and help them out.

IN SUMMARY

As mobile devices continue to make inroads into enterprise technology deployments, there will be an ever-increasing need to provide training for these applications and mobile services. This should not be considered an additional burden but rather an opportunity to change the perception of the learning and development team in your organization, offering a direct path to add value to the rest of the company.

There are some in the learning industry who shy away from these enterprise system builds and leave content generation to the development teams. While this may be a result of culture clashes or an inability to come together on team roles and delegated responsibilities, put an end to it. With the rapid cycles in the mobile market and the speed at which learners expect their content to be delivered, we cannot continue building documentation and training for custom applications in the same old way. Mobile applications should be simple enough to use without much explanation. This much is true and is documented in not only many books on the subject but also the actual documentation for the development toolkits themselves. You don't want software on your mobile phone that you must be trained to use.

That said, there is a huge opportunity for learning and development departments to lend their expertise in explaining the *why* concerning an application, not just the *how* or the *what* regarding the use of the software itself. Teach the user the advantages of learning and mastering the process and its background. How will this tool help them to do their job better? What is the result of that increase in productivity or boost in effectiveness?

Placing a solid foundation behind the tool provides a manifold boost to the overall bottom line of the company as well. More engaged, knowledgeable workers are better for the financials of the company, and they are also a lot more fun to be around.

EIGHT

CONTENT TYPE #3 DETAIL – CUSTOM LEARNING MADE POSSIBLE BY MOBILE

A BRAVE NEW WORLD

Mobile devices have opened up so many avenues for us as users. We can access our contacts, friends and family at the push of a button. We can access our email and other message formats like instant messaging (IM) while away from our computers. We have the whole of the Internet just one swipe away. This is truly amazing when you consider just how quickly it's come along.

While the smartphone has been around since the advent of Black-Berries, the Palm Treo and early Windows phone-enabled personal digital assistants (PDAs) in the late 1990s, they never caught on quite as well as the modern touch-screen devices everyone carries these days, but why? Cost, size, connectivity or a number of other stumbling blocks could have contributed to this. Ease of use instantly comes to mind, given that many original smartphone operating systems (OSs) were either desktop programs scaled down to a smaller screen or were PDA OSs migrated over to a communication device. Neither change went over big with consumers. Appeals to device speed and power also factor in, as we have long been under the impression that the faster the chip or the more RAM, the better. After a little time these marketing approaches were weeded out of smartphone promotional materials in a way that let people focus on the features of the device. Interestingly, as the power of these devices has increased and features have stabilized, marketing departments are once again trotting out the specs of a device as key selling points. These are all pieces of a puzzle answering why it took until 2011 for smartphones to outsell flip phones and feature phones (*2012 Mobile Future*, 2012, p. 10).

One aspect of the puzzle that is often overlooked is a basic concept – device capabilities.

Previous-generation smartphones lacked true mapping services, accessible app markets, decent cameras, media-handling capabilities, useful amounts of device storage and powerful, fast data networks. All these features are now readily available and came along with the current generation of touchscreen-based devices that virtually eradicated the PDA from our collective memory. The current-generation devices have overtaken the point-and-shoot camera as the most popular tool for posting photographs on Flickr. There is no doubt that smartphones have put a dent in the wallets of dedicated GPS manufacturers. According to the Swedish analysis firm, Berg Insight, "the number of mobile subscribers using a turn-by-turn navigation app or service on their handset doubled in 2011 and reached 130 million worldwide." These numbers are expected to reach 340 million by 2016 (*Global PND Shipments*, 2012).

These amazing capabilities are reasons that mLearning is getting so much attention these days. As a method of learning and development, mLearning has been around since the late 1990s, based on the work of mobile-learning pioneers such as Mike Sharples, Judy Brown, David Metcalf and Clark Quinn. With the addition of these new device features, many of the visionary notions that these and other thinkers predicted are now coming to fruition.

Consider "augmented reality" for a moment. The term was coined by Boeing employee Tom Caudell back in the 1990s, but it rose to prominence in the mid-2000s with popular YouTube video demos, then moved into mainstream marketing with a burst of activity from 2007 to 2008 via Flash mini-sites. It didn't hit the mobile apps space with any amount of fanfare until 2009 with Urbanspoon's scope feature and later with the Layar app and platform. This was roughly six years after initial discussions of augmented reality as a mobile learning tool and 15-20 years after its origins as a method for workers to assemble electrical wires inside aircrafts (Chen, 2009). That's quite a lead time. GPS applications like turn-by-turn directions and geofencing (a geofence is a virtual perimeter for a real-world geographic area) have similar stories. All great ideas, but they required a significant amount of lead time for deployment on any significant scale.

Now that a large number of device features – including Bluetooth, Wi-Fi, multitouch and gesture input, high-quality cameras, GPS, ambient light sensors, accelerometers and gyroscopes – are standard, and many more are becoming common – such as near-field communications (NFC), high-speed Bluetooth, and facial and object recognition at the OS level – we are seeing an explosion of innovation. Many of our favorite apps, games and even websites use these tools for everyday functions including sharing photos, shopping, getting directions, and even obtaining instructions for installing and leveling a shelf. These basic-use cases involve inputs and outputs, interaction models and more that simply are not possible with a desktop or laptop learning experience, and even just a few short years ago, that couldn't have been imagined by anyone but the most forward-thinking futurists.

Direct interaction between the learner and the instructional designer is seldom used in any eLearning. The online courseware we know is usually a read-only experience, with built-in assessments or scenarios that assist with the learning, but they include little or no server-side interaction (besides communication with the LMS) and almost never allow for user peer-to-peer communication or content creation for later use. The world of mobile changes this. It's certain that a mobile app will have Web connectivity at one point or another in order to provide contextual content at the point of need.

You will need to prepare yourself. Rich interactivity is something your learners have come to expect on their mobile devices. The locus of control is shifting. You are still the expert and have great input on guiding the hand of the user, but with these new devices, you must expect that the learners may be creating just as much as they are consuming.

USE OF GEOLOCATION

It's 3 p.m. on a Monday. Do you know where you are? No? (Hint: You were supposed to say you are at work.) Even if you don't know, your phone does. You might not think much about this anymore, but it's actually a big deal. Only five years ago, you needed to print directions or carry a map with you in order to pinpoint your location or access useful directions when you needed them. This required forethought. Where were you going to go? When might you head there? Were you going to drive or use public transit or walk?

Today none of these concerns really matter at all if you have a GPS-enabled smartphone or tablet. The use of GPS to determine where you are and what is around you is a common use case in everything from the mobile versions of Google Maps to social networks like Foursquare. These services can be used for a lot more than just getting directions to the nearest coffee shop and checking in once you get there. These superficialities are certainly fun, but they don't contribute to your intellectual well-being or your continued professional development. They are only a fraction of the interactions you can have with the world around you, now that your mobile device knows where you are.

A few areas where location-based services could directly impact your learning audience include:

- Directions and navigational services;

- Use of geofences or telematics;

- Route logging and efficiency tracking;

- Direction and wayfinding beyond urban settings;

- Augmented reality to give information on your surroundings; and

- Information geocaching and other assets.

Getting directions from your present location to a job site or from your client's office to the next stop on your weekly rounds is a useful capability to have with you at all times. Combine these basic navigational services with reminders or tie-ins to your CRM and perhaps an objection-handling wizard to help you cover any remaining sales obstacles. The real power of learning with navigation is the integration with other services. Consider how useful Yelp, Urbanspoon or FindMyTap can be. They not only tell you where something is and how to get there, but also give you photos, menus and – in the case of FindMyTap – which craft brews are currently on draft. Mobile learning can be delicious!

Here is a common user interface design pattern used for basic geolocation and displaying metadata about the site in the same view:

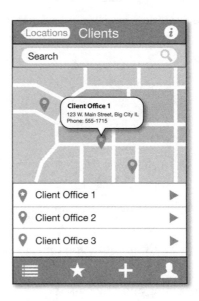

Just think for a moment about all that you may need to do when you get to your office or your mobile job site. Furthermore, how many of these tasks could be augmented by offering helpful reminders about actions or steps you need to take when you get within range of a location. This technique, known as geofencing, applies a virtual boundary line or radius around a real-world location. This is at the core of the telematics industry, commonly used with vehicle actions or operations, but it will also have a wide range of implications for learning.

Julie Schmit (2008) reported in *USA Today* that a number of logistics-focused businesses were initiating route plans to maximize fuel efficiency by limiting the number of routes, grouping packages and reducing the number of left turns made by drivers. These help to reduce fuel usage in a mileage-heavy industry where fuel costs can easily take up to 8-10 percent of revenues. Now, even if you are not delivering packages, there's probably a lot you can learn by using GPS with your mobile pros. What is the average time on site for top agents? Compared to an underperformer, how many stops does a good agent make in a day? These seem more focused on operation than learning, but when you approach these numbers from a behavioral-modeling perspective, you are merely creating profiles to determine what may need to be trained or unlearned.

In the right setting, wayfinding and augmented reality can come together in a powerful way. When I was 18, I took a tour through Gettysburg. The guide for my tour group was an expert and delivered an account of this historic site. While I had this tremendous asset at my side, helping me understand what had happened, I also observed a number of unattended people in the battlefield, touring with tattered pamphlets in hand. Fast-forward to today and you can have a GPS-enabled app guide you through the site, giving you insights from an encyclopedic source. Now there are a number of augmented reality apps that also allow you to travel back in time to experience a city as it evolved through the years. The History Pin app (http://www.historypin.com/app/) does just that. You can see today and yesteryear all mashed up in the same view via an augmented-reality overlay.

The use of augmented reality in mobile learning is really just getting started, and geolocation paired with these capabilities is turning a few heads. The Layar platform, for example, easily and inexpensively allows augmented reality to be blended into custom applications. This technology would have taken thousands of hours to develop independently. Having these platforms available for licensing in your learning applications is a boon. I dare you to look at this augmented-reality overlay in a job site performance support application, and tell me that it's not useful:

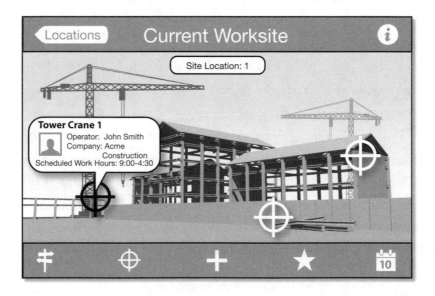

With more than 1.6 million geocaches published on geocaching websites according to the activity's Wikipedia page (*Geocaching*), it can be seen that this is a weekend hobby for many people. These caches may be logbooks or trinkets. What about using a stash, but with digital assets and information? A large manufacturing facility could have dozens of digital training caches positioned next to pieces of equipment, offering just-in-time access to manuals and up-to-date station bulletins. Planted crops could have product brochures and agronomic data made available as you approach the site. These caches could be hidden or disabled in the apps or via websites until the users draw near, ensuring only the most current information is displayed. Additional verification tools such as QR codes or augmented reality markers could be colocated with the GPS coordinates, providing an additional level of verification to prevent would-be digital asset thieves.

AUGMENTED REALITY

We've already covered location-specific augmented reality, but what about augmented reality for objects and instances away from the real world? The use of markers and other non-location specific augmented reality is exciting, too.

Technicians, inspectors, field representatives and claims agents are a few among the many who could benefit from non-locational augmented reality. Locational augmented reality is similar in many regards to the concept of virtual reality (VR) panoramas, and non-locational is akin to virtual reality objects from several years ago. What does this mean? As with VR panoramas, where the interactivity and content overlays were unique to or specific to the setting depicted, the use of locational augmented reality is concerned with exploring the space in the user's current field of vision. If you contrast this with the object VR movies we are accustomed to seeing used as product tours, walk-around inspection tools and other interactive product demonstrations, then non-locational augmented reality experiences are mostly about the specifics of an object rather than a place.

These experiences can be tremendously useful for repair personnel, field technicians, inspectors, mechanics or any other technical professionals that need just-in-time performance support in relation to real-world objects or products. Through the use of augmented reality markers, QR codes and other forms of computer vision such as pattern or object detection, it would be possible to develop a custom augmented reality application or reader experience for virtually any product in existence.

There are already a number of experiments in the works that have received some notice. A publicized proof of concept from BMW in 2007 showed a technician being aided by a pair of augmented reality goggles in order to perform engine maintenance (video uploaded by V431, 2007). The Google Glasses project focusing on augmented reality glasses received quite a buzz in the spring of 2012. While taking criticism about their aesthetic, there is no doubt that their introduction is going to shape many industries, with multitudes of potential applications for use in help and technician systems.

Consider, for a moment, what an augmented-reality system could look like as a smartphone app for a repair technician – in this case, a lineman for a telecom company (see next page).

This is just one possibility in one field. The reality is that the implementations that hit the business world will be far more interesting and varied.

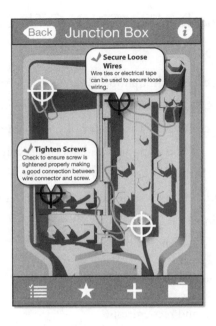

Sample augmented reality performance support app

The actual implementations in the wild thus far have largely just been experiments or only served demonstration or entertainment purposes. Many of the most popular demos rely on high-contrast augmented reality markers. They share a similar appearance to QR codes but have a bit more flexibility due to their more customizable configuration and design. Like QR codes, they are generally either black and white or otherwise similarly contrasting, and they still have a highly geometric look to them even after the customization. This is largely due to the overall crudeness of our current state of technology in image and pattern recognition. Expect to see this change as our systems grow more and more sophisticated.

It's clear that we are just getting started in augmented reality.

THE CAMERA(S) AND OTHER SENSORS

It's the enemy of every technophobe. Buying a phone without a camera today is not as easy as it sounds. A camera in a phone has become pervasive and is considered a must-have by most buyers. The camera is obviously great at taking photos and shooting videos, but there are more functions than that. Furthermore, the camera is just one new input that is available on these devices. Let's consider what you can do today with audio/visual inputs when coupled with custom development or the use of existing mobile apps:

- Computer vision;

- Facial detection and recognition;

- Augmented reality (covered in the previous section);

- QR codes;

- Voice detection;

- Voice control;

- Dictation; and

- Other audio recognition.

Computer vision is a rapidly evolving area of development. The basics are these: an imaging sensor takes in an image, and software algorithms that perform edge detection, blob detection, and motion sensing are applied. Via tuning and various pre-defined patterns, assorted objects can be detected. These detections can be simplistic

– like recognizing that something is blue or red – or more complicated – like distinguishing letters and words. A high-profile launch of the application WordLens in 2010 exhibited this functionality and went several steps further by not only recognizing words, but also sending them to a translation API and altering the image a user saw to the newly translated version. Does it sound like magic? That's exactly how it felt when I used it.

With many books and dissertations written in this area alone, computer vision is a broad subject. In simple terms, here's how shape or object detection works (based on the steps of Canny edge detection):

Step 1: Original image

Step 2: Reduce noise from the image

Step 3: Determine edge strength and direction

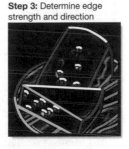

Step 4: Apply nonmaximum suppression

Step 5: Final output

Computer vision is typically achieved through an image-processing algorithm that uses a multi-stage process to determine the edges of objects by comparing bordering pixels with surrounding areas. One example of this is Canny edge detection, named for the inventor of the algorithm, John Canny (1986). Using additional algorithms then allows more patterns to be made from the edge-based ones, tying the results to items remembered as real-world equivalents via arrays or other database storage and retrieval methods. Once the object has been detected, other programmatic logic can then be applied, allowing the learner to take cues or receive just-in-time updates about the action or scene at hand.

Facial detection and recognition is a subarea of this discipline, and lots of applications on your mobile phone are already using it. It's built into your mobile phone camera, allowing you to take better pictures of your subjects. The Android platform also has a number of handsets that can be unlocked when a face is detected. There are a few emerging APIs that third parties can integrate into their existing apps for adding this feature. For example, the software at http://face.com/ is one such licensable platform with available APIs for both iOS and Android platforms.

Augmented reality would not be possible without a camera. It's such a large field that I'm actually going to pass on talking about it for now and cover it in the next section.

By now, almost everyone knows about QR codes. A QR or quick response code is a square-shaped, bi-color, blocky graphic image that a QR reader application can use to perform a number of functions. QR codes were first created in 1994 by DENSO WAVE (*About QRcode. com*). The current incarnation of QR code can be used to encode more information and be recognized with more fidelity than it was able to in its infancy, but the basic idea is the same. Using key-identifying blocks of graphic markings, a QR code presents its reading application with a way-finding mechanism to determine the issuing body, the action the device should take after reading the code, and any metadata that is pertinent. In many regards, it's like an evolved Universal product code (UPC), just a bit denser in terms of how much information it can display. The three concentric squares in the corners of the code identify it as a QR code to the reader application.

The diagram below, adapted from Willv (2011), depicts other areas of the QR code and what they do:

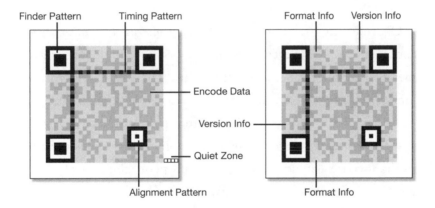

Finder Pattern – enables scanners to identify the QR Code. Alterations can prevent scanners from reading the code.

Format Info – what scanners read first as the code is deciphered. It contains the mask pattern and error-correction rate of the code.

Timing Pattern – white and black modules (pixel elements) are alternately arranged to determine the coordinates. The timing pattern is placed between two finder patterns in a QR code.

Version Info – identifies the version of the QR code. Data-storage capacity and error-correction levels vary by version.

Encoded Data – data that needs to be interpreted by the scanner.

Alignment Pattern – enables QR code scanners to correct for distortion when the code is bent or curved. Alterations to this pattern are not recommended.

Quiet Zone – space left around the QR code for optimal readability. Quiet zones are suggested to be two to four modules wide. A module is the single smallest pixel element of the QR code. (Willv, 2011).

QR codes are useful now for delivering just-in-time information and wayfinding. However, as computer vision technology improves, they will ultimately become unnecessary. The reasons for this are multifarious, but these codes are not pretty to look at, and design-conscious people will remove them from their products as soon as possible, especially since the perceived value in scanning the code to the user is relativity low, leading to a poor adoption rate. In a 2011 study by Bradley University, spearheaded by Department of Interactive Media Chairman Jim Ferolo, only 12 percent of audience members in a directed campaign responded to or used QR codes (Ferolo et. al, 2011). Other advertising modalities handily outperformed this high-tech vehicle.

Voice detection, voice control, dictation and audio recognition have huge potential for us as learning developers in interacting with our learners. The barrier to entry and interaction for users can often be the tedium experienced in using software keyboards, modalities of data entry and the expectation to open apps continually then enter the information in order to reach the desired outcome. As voice control and recognition systems continue to improve and gain acceptance, what currently seems more like a gimmick or marketing tool like

Apple's Siri will eventually become an indispensable input method for interacting with users.

There are already a few excellent examples of audio-recognition tools in the marketplace that aid in identifying sounds in your surroundings. The popular application, Shazam, for instance, helps you identify music that is playing around you. It does this with a cloud-based service that uses audio-pattern recognition against an ever-growing database of songs and artists. There is currently a project under way at the University of Wisconsin-Madison called WeBird that is working on an application like Shazam for, you guessed it, bird calls. The application uses an approach similar to Shazam or MusicID, but with a database focused on wildlife calls. The platform can currently identify a variety of bird calls, but the system can also be used for insects and other wildlife, like frogs (Barncard, 2011).

The possibilities are tremendous as, like visual cues, audio cues are a strong learning tool.

BIG DATA AND MOBILE

By many estimates, 2012 looks to be the year of big data for many industries, and learning is just getting started in this realm. Big data – the use of data sets so large that they cannot be handled via traditional database management methodologies – is a rapidly evolving field of research and applications.

As more people buy equipment capable of interfacing with information services, the datasets they interact with grow larger. This is a network-effect result, where growth is amplified and increased as more people are drawn to various platforms and interactions grow in depth and breadth.

Big data is beginning to factor heavily in many areas of our lives. Studies of our buying, driving, and all other habits are currently under way in both academic institutions and corporations. The objective of these studies is to understand our behavior patterns in order to serve and/or sell to us more effectively. In the case of several programs, the objective is to discover potential safety and civic issues in order to prevent everything from natural disasters to acts of terrorism.

Because mobile devices are always with us, contain so many sensors and inputs, and have a constant connection with the cloud, they offer a tremendous opportunity to contribute significantly to big data. Logging typical events and movements would have been a tedious affair just a handful of years ago, but at this point, there are more than 10 million Foursquare users (*10,000,000 Strong*, 2011). Additionally, 200 million monthly active users create 2 billion posts tagged with locations on Facebook, according to *Inside Facebook*'s Brittany Darwell. Facebook product manager Josh Williams announced at the Where Conference in San Francisco in April 2012 that about a quarter of Facebook users added location data to their posts each month (Darwell, 2012).

It's plain to see that mobile users have definitely become big contributors to big data with little or no effort.

These big data applications, typically powered by large, scalable cloud databases and massive infrastructures, usually have a few common characteristics:

- High availability and instant scalability;

- Large, rapidly growing customer bases and workforces;

- NoSQL or non-traditional database back ends such as MongoDB or MarkLogic; and

- A mobile-first approach to application design and development.

While at first blush these applications may not seem like part of a typical learning and development professional's toolkit, we must begin to familiarize ourselves with this area. Soon, NoSQL and mobile-first LMS/LRS systems will hit the street, and the first user-driven big data learning systems will emerge. We must be ready to understand and leverage the amount of information we will have about our learners. We will know where and when they accessed our information, what content is sticky and valuable, which content is for solitary use, and which is frequently shared. The simple approach to measurement of completion via a checkmark in an LMS report screen is not going to cut it. Real-time data, unlike any systems we currently use, will provide behavior-modeling insights in the near future.

In a small organization, it may be a bit more difficult to see how you might directly harness this for your use, but you can buy data for sectors or vertical markets similar to yours and use those to make informed decisions about your current training offerings. The numbers might not be about your learners in particular, but they are about learners who are similar to yours.

When you can predict the patterns that you will see in a newly created module, app or training service based on the exhibited behaviors of your learners, not only will you deliver more effective training, but you will also avoid overtraining. Business productivity in this post-Great Recession world is largely about doing more with less. With big data on our side, we can do just that.

IN SUMMARY

The new mobile devices have brought a wealth of technologies to us, and many of them are mobile-first technologies by nature. They were meant to be taken with us. Because of this, and because of their ease of use, it's clear to see there are many applications for them as learning tools. Everything from understanding where we are in the world and reacting to it to being able to project additional layers of data over the images in our phone is changing the way in which we interact and learn from our environment.

The mass of information out there is startling, and we really haven't seen anything yet.

NINE

CONTENT TYPE #4 DETAIL – USER-GENERATED CONTENT

MOBILE IS INTRINSICALLY SOCIAL

When you pick up your phone, often you are doing so to get information from someone else, usually through text, voice or even Web content like tweets and Facebook statuses. These bits of content are user created. They don't usually come from an authoritative source, and they are almost never run though legal first – unless you are calling your lawyer at the time, I suppose.

The point is that we carry these devices to access and retrieve information from other people, and we are always communicating. Most of the content we get comes from unofficial sources. We send or receive text messages at a rate of about 40 per day (Smith, 2011) among coworkers, friends and family. On average, smartphone users are consuming 435 MB of data per month to use Facebook, Twitter and other social media while away from home (Kellogg, 2011). Without thinking about it, we connect to a Wi-Fi network at a coffee shop or airport to get on the company wiki or check our email. We use these devices to access company knowledge networks when at a job site or on a sales call to access best practice information on the sales team blog. While we're shopping in a store, we see a product and simultaneously read its reviews on Amazon to determine whether it's worth the price.

Not one of the above examples is a learning and development-produced piece of content. You may have had a hand in shaping the delivery mechanism, and you may continue to groom and curate the content on sites and services, but you did not write all the entries on that blog or wiki. Add content types like images and videos to the mix, and you start to see where we are going with this.

The hunger and need for content from your audience far outstrips your ability to produce it all by yourself. Even if you had the largest budget in the world to produce these pieces, you would find a lack somewhere else in the learning supply chain. You wouldn't have enough subject matter experts or hours in a day, and you couldn't provide quick enough turnaround to requests – the list of issues is a long one.

The list becomes a lot shorter when you have the strength of your organization backing you. Dozens of high-performing sales reps are communicating with each other faster and with less friction than you would encounter if you had to conduct all the interviews and organize the data alone. The market is changing too quickly for 6-12-month learning product cycles. Leverage the power of your workforce, and get the message out there with greater efficiency.

The avenues are virtually limitless. One-to-one, one-to-many, many-to-one, and many-to-many – all these communication modes and more are available to you through mobile communications. You need to investigate your learners' needs for peer-based learning and social learning and get it out there in a mobile-friendly format. Easier said than done, right? Let's take a look at these types of learning deliverables and examine how to optimize them for mobile use.

INFORMAL LEARNING IS THE FUTURE

The basic concept of informal learning dates back to the early 20th century with the pioneering work of John Dewey (1859-1952) and Malcolm Knowles (1913-1997). Later, after the advent of the modern training organization and ASTD (founded in 1944), people like Ivan Illich (in his books, *Deschooling Society* and *Imprisoned in the Global Classroom*) and Jay Cross began to extol the virtue of learning outside the classroom and without a prescribed path or curriculum.

Informal learning appears to require some level of autodidacticism – or self-directed learning – and that may be true to a certain extent, because much of informal learning happens at a pace completely controlled by the motivation and timing of the learner. However, with mobile learning and the social connectivity that it affords us, informal learning may happen on mobile just by accident, because connecting with our peers is so easy. With a few apps and a level of connectivity between yourself and friends on Twitter or Facebook, it's almost impossible to avoid social learning at this time.

Even the elementary school system, secondary education, and adult and continuing education are coming under scrutiny to perform and do more with less. A quick way to add to the bottom line in your sector is to start taking advantage of this effective form of learning. According to Jay Cross (2007), it's estimated that 90 percent of adults are actively engaged in a form of informal learning. Additionally, a 1999 study from the University of Toronto found that 96% of adults had at least a little informal learning each week, and it didn't matter whether these adults had no diploma or a university degree (Livingstone). How are you using informal learning in your organization? Are you aiding it? Blocking it? Measuring it?

In the not-so-distant future, the role of informal learning will continue to blur as the next generation of learning-management systems like Project Tin Can and credentialing systems like Mozilla Badges come online. These have been designed with informal learning in mind, so adding these pervasive forms of content consumption to your overall learning toolkit will become a real possibility.

There is a long-running supposition that the basic breakdown of how learning occurs in an organization is like this:

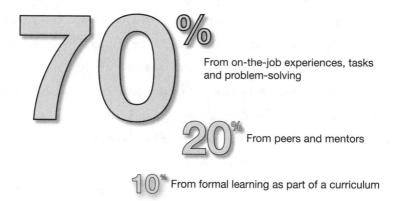

70% From on-the-job experiences, tasks and problem-solving

20% From peers and mentors

10% From formal learning as part of a curriculum

The source is undocumented, and its accuracy has been debated for as long as the number has been out in the public eye. This will probably continue, because it is unlikely that anyone can prove or disprove this metric with any real certainty. The source is not quite as clear as it could be, but the breakdown works like this:

- 10% – Formal learning as part of a curriculum;

- 20% – Learning via your peers and mentoring; and

- 70% – Informal learning via your peers and coworkers.

Even if the numbers are off by 10-20% or even more, there is still significant work that can be done to help your organization via mobile learning and with it, informal learning.

How can we do this? Let's examine a few methods. You may be using a sample of these in your organization already.

WIKIS

Many companies have a form of wiki in place. This may be a true wiki built on a dedicated wiki platform like MediaWiki, PhpWiki, and Wiki-Spaces, or it may be a system built on top of Microsoft SharePoint or other enterprise-collaboration platforms such as Atlassian's Confluence.

There have been a number of successful case studies written about using wikis for corporate and informal learning, one of the better examples being the well-known Intelpedia. With more than 25,000 entries in the system dating back to 2008 and more than 500 pages of edits happening daily, it's easy to see why this has become a cornerstone of the social or informal learning system for Intel.

Here is a list of what's great about a corporate wiki:
- You are always working with the current version of the content.
- Diverse talent can be leveraged for contributions, regardless of the location.

- Changes can be controlled with user permissions.
- Mistakes (and even vandalism) can be reversed easily by rolling back to a previous version of the content.
- It is accessible anywhere via a Web browser (for viewing and editing).
- Most wikis do not require any knowledge of HTML.
- The page history and recent changes are tracked, and most wikis provide a mechanism to send proactive change notifications.
- Most wikis have talk, discussion, or comment pages where debates about tough issues can occur before deciding how best to revise controversial pages. (Foster, 2006).

The advantages listed on this page are spot on. Keep in mind that these systems are typically not mobile-friendly right out of the box. The average wiki theme has three columns and often uses a small font size. These systems are designed for high-resolution Web browsers and focus on content density, not chunking. As you know by now, these design cues are not the best for creating a stellar mobile user interface and in turn an engaging mobile-learning user experience.

Many of these wiki platforms do have a few mobile-friendly themes or templates available, and the others are at least customizable enough that if you have a Web designer on staff and a software license that allows for modifications to the wiki code, you should mark this project on your radar.

Consider for a second a typical wiki design:

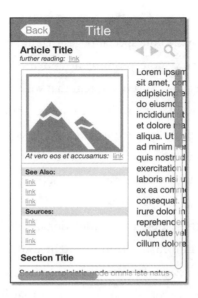

Now take a look at a more mobile-friendly adaptation of that same wiki page when a small amount of work is done on the design theme:

The differences are marked. We've removed the multi-column layout and most of the links to the special pages that are typical of wikis. The search feature is now more prominent, and much of the screen real estate focuses on a curated list of content that we have chosen to feature.

In a more advanced system, similar curated content could be auto-generated, or an analytics-generated list of links that refreshes based on the user's past access could be provided. Perhaps the most popular pages in the system by access count, talk activity, or edit count could be displayed.

Regardless of these design considerations, wikis are still a highly useful social and informal learning-content tool and should be revitalized with fresh designs for smartphones and the new needs of the mobile workforce. A properly equipped wiki that has been formatted for mobile use could get a new lease on life.

KNOWLEDGE BASES

Many people mistake knowledge bases for wikis or other databases containing information for retrieval, though there are key distinctions that you should be aware of as a learning and development professional:

- Knowledge base systems are usually only concerned with a specific ontology. Wikis can often be much more generalized.

- Wikis are only for human consumption, while knowledge bases can often be used by computers in a logic-chain or deductive-reasoning process for troubleshooting or support.

- Knowledge bases are typically question/answer driven (such as a

FAQ). Wikis are usually topic and title driven.

- Knowledge bases can be browsed via a directory or menu system, whereas wikis are nearly always browsed via searches and inline links inside of search term entries.

The usual multi-column layouts and heavy use of categorized branching are two similarities that wikis and knowledge bases share. It's because of this that to make a user-friendly, mobile knowledge base, you would make many of the same changes that you would to a wiki.

Knowledge Bases	Wikis
Specific ontology	General taxonomy
Human and computer users	Human users
Driven by Q&A	Driven by topics, titles, search
Equally browsed and searched	Primarily searched

This table clearly shows the differences and similarities between a knowledge-base system and a wiki:

Here are several points to keep in mind as you move a knowledge base to a mobile-friendly implementation:

- Because wikis are concerned with a specific body of knowledge and may have users who are familiar with this on a deeper level than most users of a wiki might be, consider your chunking and browsing use cases carefully. You'll want clear categorization and an easy-to-use drop-down menu or a branching structure that's readily exposed to help with navigation.

- Because knowledge bases may be machine-read with deductive reasoning, workflows or chained to if/then/else types of outcomes, consider how you can make your content available via SMS or other quick-query-friendly systems. Don't require your users to browse when they can ask.

- Don't forget to provide related questions or the next steps for your users. Since users on the road might not know what they need to know to complete the next steps in a task while your system might, make available recommended content for those who may be continuing a workflow or series of tasks.

- Provide categories and subcategories for your mobile-enabled knowledge bases, because long, scrolling Web pages on a mobile browser are difficult to use, and most mobile Web browsers lack the find-in-page feature that many power users employ for long lists in a Web page.

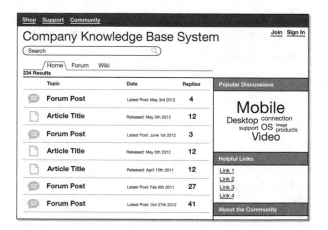

Take a look below at a common type of interface design for a knowledge base system on a desktop computer Web browser:

You can see right off the bat that the multi-column layout will have to go. You can also see just how much space is wasted in the design for extras such as navigating to non-knowledge-base content and niceties like tag clouds. The prominence and placement of user forums here is also problematic because they are also not as useful as authoritative content, and users will not be as apt to enter discussions while on the go. They will want to get their answers and be on with their days.

The same page, when slightly tweaked for use on a smartphone,

instantly becomes more user-friendly. Check out this simple one-column design and the cleverly tucked away drop-down menu in the upper-left corner.

Knowledge bases have long been a staple in the technician and call center support staff's arsenal of help and just-in-time information. Just because we are now moving to mobile doesn't mean we need to abandon these sources. On the contrary these volumes of curated and rated content are ever more valuable now that we can apply their information at the point of need and use them to finish tasks easier and faster.

SOCIAL LEARNING

Social learning is an emerging area in organizations that is focused on the use of social tools like blogs, microblogging, and social networks to connect colleagues and share knowledge in a low-friction manner. While this seems new, we have always been socially learning at work. Every office has that go-to person on a given subject. You may hear, "Jennifer knows that system well; go ask her," and "Well, Bob is out of town on vacation, so no one can fix that problem right now." Social learning tools and systems are typically put in place to remedy these issues.

I frequently use a statement when speaking with my colleagues and clients about mobile and social: "Mobile is intrinsically social, and social is intrinsically mobile."

When you think about it, this is the epitome of truth regarding mobile learning. Mobile devices were originally made for communication. They are and always have been social devices. Social media and networking since the earliest days of Friendster and Orkut have always been about letting your friends or contacts know what you are up to, where you are going, what you just did, or what you are about to do.

With the rise of smartphones and tablets, and the continued progress of modern social networks and other location-based services, social media has only become more relevant. With every new feature and network that appear, there are new ways to store and share your knowledge and more ways to learn from others in your social and personal learning network.

Consider for a moment the way you learn now compared to the way you learned even five years ago. You no doubt check your social networks either right before or right after you check your email and probably before you read any Web news at large. If something happened while you were away from your computer or while you had your phone tucked away, then there is a good chance that you will hear about it on your social networks before you see it on the television or by visiting a proper news site.

Services such as Twitter and Facebook are great for public or non-work-related content and do have one or two functions for learning professionals as well, but now there are many more avenues that you can go down with regard to making your corporate-learning network a social-learning network. With services and sites like Yammer, Jive, and Saltbox making social learning a reality in the enterprise, each of them with extensive mobile integration, you have no excuses left. These networks can be integrated with your single-sign-on and security policies. Usually they can be hosted either on premises or via a software-as-a-service (SaaS) or cloud arrangement.

The bottom line is this: people learn from other people, via examples and discussion. Conversation is a powerful learning tool. This is made possible in mobile via social learning tools like social networks and messaging. The more focused social tools you can provide to your users when they are on the go, the more they will tap into their personal and social learning networks while away from their desks.

liot Masie Learning TRENDS site distributed a survey in 2010 about companies and their interest in and use of social learning. The numbers were overwhelming. More than 76 percent of companies surveyed either had or planned to have social learning in place for their employees. Ninety percent of them were using it to teach employees from the experiences of others. More than one-third of them (35 percent) were looking to use it to decrease formal learning time. Most of the time, these social learning efforts were centered on collaborative documents and systems like wikis (76 percent), but more than 67 percent of these efforts also had an internal social network component as well (Masie, 2010).

If you are in the majority of companies already using social learning in your organization, but haven't yet made it available for mobile users, you should ask, "Why not?"

REVIEWS AND RECOMMENDATION ENGINES

The concept of adding reviews, comments and discussion in a learning system is not new. Academic-focused LMS solutions like Blackboard and Moodle, along with many other large enterprise LMS variants such as Saba, Plateau and SumTotal, have had these as features for some time now. The real power in using this data ultimately lies in what you do with it.

Already I've spoken at length about curation and careful content selection in this book, but it just keeps popping up. Mobile devices are somewhat limited in their capabilities, as already noted. Recognizing and providing the most applicable content to the learners at their moments of need is our job as instructional designers and information architects.

We can continue to do this manually. It's worked thus far, right? To answer that question, I like this quote from well-known management consultant Donald Tapscott:

> In the old economy it was, "if it ain't broke, don't fix it;" well, in the new economy, "if it ain't broke, you need to break it before your competition does." So innovation drives everything. (Tapscott, Ticoll & Lowy, 2000).

The time has come to put new systems in place that help us manage our information better. If you or your learning and development department have been through a training-needs analysis lately, I'm sure you've noticed something. There is a possible knowledge gap in your current offerings and the amount of content your learners need in order to do their jobs. Compare the most recent training-needs analysis to the one that preceded it, and that one to the analysis before it. Is the gap shrinking or widening?

Because the gap is likely widening, it leaves you with more training materials to produce, curate, deploy, and maintain. In turn, this requires you to continue making this content available to your learners and marketing it. This is a no-win situation for you and them. How can you expose this important information to your audience without continually blasting them with email newsletters and announcements (which have a limited success rate anyway)?

One answer to this is a recommendation engine or system. If you shop at Amazon, watch Netflix or use TiVo, or have ever used music apps like Last.fm, Spotify or Pandora, then you are probably already familiar with this method. The benefit of these systems from a commerce point of view is obvious. You can expose new products or services to buyers based on past purchases, viewing history, and interactions with content on the site. This is usually done with algorithms developed specifically for the site, and in the case of Amazon, it's the foundation of the business itself.

These systems usually function with one of a few different methods. One common way is that the system uses relational metadata to note the characteristics of content items or products that the buyer either purchases or views independent of others on the site or using the service. This content-based approach to filtering and recommendations tailors the content specifically to the user. This type of filtering helps to provide deeper access to features that the users have already stated they like, and it enhances reinforcement techniques to dig deeper into a particular subject area. I would consider this a great approach to creating a learning path where users are attempting to build mastery in a particular skill set or area.

Another common way that these systems behave is to cross-reference user behavior with that of other site users. This can create a commonality or provide recommendations based on what others like that you have viewed, interacted with or also liked. This is a more collaborative style or approach and works well to aid in discovery. By providing wayfinding to content that may have previously remained undiscovered, you are encouraging users to explore what they wouldn't have found in a systematic way. I would suggest this kind of approach when attempting to do cross-training.

Many of these recommendation engines are just now beginning to trickle into the learning and open-source communities. If you are interested in implementing such a system and your current learning platform doesn't have something like this available, then I would recommend reading about the progress of open recommendation engines at sites such as Mendeley or the numerous efforts outlined in Toby Segaran's 2007 book, *Programming Collective Intelligence: Building Smart Web 2.0 Applications.*

When you consider that usage patterns and content preferences as well as mobile-specific contexts like location, device type, and data speed can help inform content recommendations, you have the foundation for a highly personalized learning experience.

GATHERING AND DISTRIBUTING INFORMATION WITH A MOBILE DEVICE

Most of the content strategies we have discussed thus far have been about consumption of information. While many of us spend the bulk of our time on our mobile devices taking in content, these can also be great content creation tools as well. Let's not forget that they do have live Web connections and highly capable Web browsers. When you add apps to the equation, the possibilities for content creation and sharing as a form of mobile social learning is multiplied.

There is a variety of tools on most mobile devices for use in data-gathering and input. What are the most common tools available today? We covered a few of these in the previous chapter due to their uniquely mobile capabilities. Consider these for use in peer-based and social learning, informal learning, and user-generated content:

- High megapixel still cameras;

- High-definition video cameras;

- Microphone;

- Brightness sensors;

- Internal storage and file systems;

- Orientation sensors and accelerometers; and

- Other assorted sensors – compasses, GPS, thermometers,

Input Methods	Web	App
High-megapixel still cameras	○	●
High-definition video camera	○	●
Microphone	○	●
Brightness sensors	○	● Some can access
Internal storage and file systems	●	●
Orientation sensors and accelerometers	● Simple orientation data only	●
Other assorted sensors - Compasses, GPS, thermometer, barometer, altimeter	○ GPS only (users must allow access)	● Sensors vary by platform

barometers, altimeters and more.

These can be used via applications, and most can be accessed either directly or indirectly via Web browsers. This table outlines the input methods and their accessibility in apps or browsers as well as the type of media, data or other information that you can typically access as a designer or developer.

All too often we expect learners on the go to read from data stores and interact with learning apps on a superficial level. We may do this out of fear of alienating our less-savvy users, or perhaps we afraid to lose control over the information in our systems. These fears are largely unfounded.

In February 2011, media sharing service Pixable calculated that 60 billion photos had been uploaded to Facebook by the end of 2010. With about 6 billion photos being uploaded each month, it was estimated the total number would reach 100 billion by the summer of 2011. This is clearly a content-creation task. Pixable also found in its sample of 100,000 users that "older people upload as many photos" as younger people, though "photo tags begin to decline among users in their late 20s" (Natalie, 2011). This is surprising considering the typical view that older users (35+ years) are not able or do not desire to interact on these systems in a content-creation-type role. Even more striking is the total number of smartphone users that accessed or interacted with Facebook on their mobile devices. Benedict Evans from Enders Analysis discovered that as of December 2011, 300 million (40 percent) monthly active users accessed Facebook through a mobile device. This may be the last known data, as Evans noted in an April 2012 update that Facebook has stopped disclosing its app information (Evans, 2011). These public numbers make it apparent that many people are comfortable with creating content on their mobile phones.

The other fear – that abuse will occur when users can upload or edit content on a work-based learning resource or portal – is also unfounded. The previously mentioned Intelpedia has not experienced spamming or vandalism. Josh Bancroft, the Intelpedia manager, told JD Lasica in 2010:

> In the four-plus years that Intelpedia has been up and running, I have had exactly zero reported instances of an unwanted edit – of someone spamming or vandalizing or doing something inappropriate. (Lasica, 2010).

This fear is not mobile-specific but applies to all user-generated content. However, because mobile devices are as secure as typical intranet-accessing PCs (if not more so), and we can identify any user that enters data, this fear is just as unfounded as it was years ago.

Content creation on mobile devices is just getting started. With the billion-dollar purchase of Instagram by Facebook in April 2012, it's clear that there is something to it.

IN SUMMARY

Mobile and social learning are closely linked at the lowest levels. The same device you use to talk or message with your friends and colleagues can be the same device you use to read and learn or that helps you navigate or create new materials.

With a little work, wikis and knowledge bases originally created in the PC era are just as mobile friendly as any other mobile-first system. You will need to rethink your approach to interfaces, but it's also an exercise in content curation and providing new social tools to help the most useful content bubble up.

You will need to integrate reviews and recommendations as your mobile content base grows. It may be the only way to spread content governance duties around and ensure the most important content is found in the thickets of user-generated media.

Speaking of user-generated content from mobile users, be sure to offer opportunities to the users to contribute via their mobile devices, not just the desktop PC. Advanced-media creation on the mobile device will likely require moving your content from a mobile Web interface to a dedicated app, but as security sandboxes for mobile browsers are relaxed, this will change.

TEN

TAKING ACTION AND STARTING PROJECTS

TURNING YOUR STRATEGY INTO REALITY

At last, here we are! This is where the talking ends and the action starts. You know you have to get something out to your learners. You even know what it is. It might be an app, maybe an SMS service or even a website for your tablet users. Whatever the end deliverable you have in mind, you will need to do a little groundwork to get the ball rolling.

You need supporters, team members, and external stakeholders. You also need an instructional design methodology and a development process. You must establish goals, deadlines and scope in order to stay in your allocated budget – Oh yeah. That. A budget. You'll need one of those, too.

Meanwhile, you are bound to have external stakeholders and other market forces like your competition breathing down your neck.

So what are you waiting for? Let's get started and build something already! I'm not going to lie - it's probably going to be a bumpy ride for you. Anything worth doing usually is. So let's get ready to do the following:

- Establish a budget and schedule;

- Establish scope;

- Set up a team;

- Maintain velocity and meet our deadlines; and

- Learn new development methodologies.

Once we have these parameters in place we can move on to design and development. For now, let's complete the items on the above list.

ESTABLISHING BUDGETS AND SCHEDULES

I wrestled with the order of this sequence: budget, schedule and scope.

Consider this for a moment: Does the business case or need determine the project's ultimate scope, or should the scope change to meet the budget and schedule? The probable answer is, "It depends." For the sake of argument and the need to set a stake in the ground somewhere, it's best to conclude that more often than not the project's scope is dictated by a budget rather than the other way around. There are certainly exceptions to this when the product's core features or the business case takes precedence, but let's get serious. When was the last time you heard management say, "Money is no object; solve this problem!"?

In my experience, the key limiting factor of a project's overall boundaries is the budget. Without that, you have no project. Have you ever allocated resources to a project that had no budget? It might float off the radar for a little while, but that is rare and almost never leads to success. Your budget could be comprised of a couple key elements, but they all boil down to one: available funding to pay for the costs incurred to complete the work.

You need to establish the overall cost you are willing to undertake for this project. Costs may include internal or external resources, hardware or software, etc. Monetary costs should not be considered the only way to establish a budget. Any properly formed budget needs to take into account risk management. A contingency needs to be in place to manage matters when something goes, "Kablooie!" You are likely not equipped to do risk analysis all on your own, so involve someone from accounting, HR, procurement or other departments that are familiar with costing for resources, human or otherwise.

Your people have hourly costs. There are also hidden costs and maybe even opportunity costs that are incurred by moving resources from one project to another. Last time I checked, we can't yet clone our teammates, so when you move someone off one project to work somewhere else, the other project incurs extra costs because that person must be replaced. You need to plan for this.

Licensing software, purchasing new technology, and covering support agreements – all need to be planned ahead of time if you want to avoid surprises. Will you need to train your staff? Will you need to form an RFP committee or process? Evaluate vendors? These take time and money. Don't get caught off guard as you're going in.

With the budget established, use it as a key element of your work plan. Don't create a budget and put it in a dark hole to die. Refer to it as your mobile development project unfolds to track costs incurred against it, maintain your schedule, and stay within scope. This doesn't matter if you are building it yourself or have a vendor building it. You may have a flat fee to pay your vendor, but you don't treat the rest of your budget like it's a blank check. Every time you get on the phone, have a meeting, schedule another round of testing, or review documents for a project, you are drawing from that budget. Track your own time on the product's development or face the consequences once it comes time to account for the work and effort spent to produce the end result.

After the budget is established and you have costed your resources properly, you will likely have a portion of time for the project that you can draw on. How long can a project last with the budget and size of the team you have allocated? When is the event, conference, or product launch happening that needs the content you are producing? There are probably other resources you are going to need in order to reverse engineer a salient, achievable schedule. Once you have an end date in mind, it's good to work backwards from that appointment to determine the times for intermediary milestones and deliverables. Do not frivolously throw these dates out. You must be conservative in your planning and talk with the personnel you are counting on. After doing this, determine if the dates you have set are realistic. A great way to start your project on the wrong foot is to miss your first milestone or flub your deliverable dates. Be diligent and scope the intermediary milestones appropriately in order to set your team up for success.

That leads us to the next topic – scoping your efforts to meet the budget and schedule.

ESTABLISHING SCOPE

The project's scope is likely to be a function of the budget combined with a basic business case for the application. After all, without a limiting factor like budget, your scope could be infinite, right? Likewise with schedule – you must launch something. You have to reach your audience by a certain date or event. Hence, you have a need for a realistic schedule given your product's scope.

Even with the best of intentions and planning, it's likely you will encounter a little scope creep when you begin work.

Scope creep is generally acknowledged as massively bad. Have you ever heard it mentioned in the same breath as what we like about projects? Does it ever occur due to proper planning and following that plan? No. So why is it so often a part of our work flow? Why do so many of your projects suffer from scope creep?

I conducted an unscientific poll one day on Twitter about why scope creep happens. The basic trends in the responses emerged:

- Lack of understanding of user requirements;

- Stakeholders being out of the loop during the establishment of the scope; and

- Inability to say "no" as requests come in.

Let's talk about that first one. In Chapters Two and Four we talked about audience needs and how to gather them, but what if you can't properly obtain end-user requirements? What happens when you don't know your audience?

Often we don't consider the users' actual goals and end up designing the work from our idealized view of how everything should be, not taking into account the true context in which the content will be used. Consider a mobile application created in a vacuum with little consideration for the user's situation. An application that makes it all the way through the design phase and into development without this vital step will need additional revisions and features added. If you fail to understand design and technical needs, then this will result in a debt that will have to be paid when the goals and needs of the user are finally uncovered.

What are design and technical debt? As we create a solution that's expected to meet a specific goal, we make sacrifices along the way. An example of a design debt might be the lack of a flexible navigation system. A technical debt might be that the team has not adequately planned to create an object-oriented approach to the project, resulting in wasted programming effort. Whatever those debts may be, they need to be paid back as change requests occur.

Design and technical debt are not scope changes, but they make it tougher to respond to future changes with agility. Because this debt almost always occurs to a small degree, it's linked to the fact that as scope is fluid, so is the ability to make informed decisions regarding the creation of optimal solutions.

It is just as important to define what is out of scope based on requirements as it is to define what is *in* scope. This leads to a further narrowing of the cone of uncertainty and a higher chance of hitting the mark. What is the cone of uncertainty? Take a look at this example:

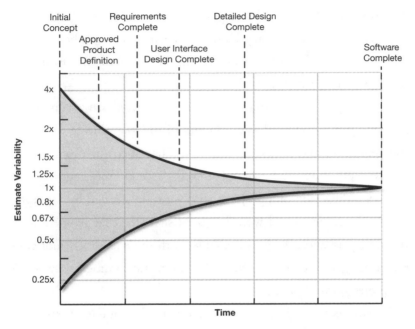

(Adapted from Atwood, 2006).

Originally conceived in 1958 by the founders of American Association of Cost Engineers, the cone has long been used to describe how the costs of a project are more variable at the beginning. As scope is determined, it becomes easier to achieve accuracy in estimates of the price or effort required to produce the work under consideration. As the project's timeline progresses, the degree of how inaccurate your estimate can be is decreased. This requires decision making and thinking critically about what is in bounds and what is out of bounds for the effort. Without this process, the cone will not narrow, and the variability of the scope will remain.

As the project is defined in the early stages, you are working to remove this scope variability and make determinations that firm up the scope and allow you as the project lead to make clearer estimates on costs and schedules. This requires a proper understanding of user requirements. This can only be done by surveying stakeholders and creating use cases and personas that line up with the needs of your users. We will cover that in Chapter 11.

According to my Twitter survey, another reason why scope creep happens is that stakeholders can be out of the loop during the establishment of a project's scope. I'm sure you have been involved in situations where you have a meeting or even a series of meetings to shape and hone the vision of a project that is set to be created by the team. A lot of great ideas and work has been shared. What happens after the group disbands? A new stakeholder with some level of seniority or budgetary power enters the fray. This interaction immediately places the project into jeopardy.

Do you recall the FedEx commercial with the conference table full of people ideating about how to save the company money? One poor office drone meekly suggests, "We could open an account on FedEx.com – save 10 percent on online express shipping." For a while, no one responds. The silver fox executive at the table sits with his brow furrowed in deep concentration before he breaks his silence, gesticulating confidently while word-for-word reiterating the same proposition. Everyone in the room but the office worker praises the executive's brilliant idea. The baffled worker argues that was exactly what he just said. The executive corrects, "No, because I *also* did this," and repeats the motion (Fed Ex stolen idea). Yeah, you don't want to be there. You owe it to yourself to keep the appropriate people engaged. Have them in the meetings, weighing in on the documents. Put questions in front of them that require their input, and lay out the consequences if they miss those dates, neglect those decisions, or overlook the opportunity for changes. There has to be accountability all around.

The last source of scope creep lies firmly in your court. You must exercise fortitude. When new requests come in, you have to be able to refuse them. Use the deadline you have established. Use the project's original goals and the user personas to put a stake in the ground. You need to adhere to your vision of a version 1.0 of the project. Changing your vision at this point will likely cause a chain reaction.

Weakness in your adherence to scope at the first onset of scope creep is a surefire way to drop blood in the water. You must stand strong. Build a great 1.0 product, and build on top of it. Take any extra feature requests and push them to a future milestone. In agile development circles, this is typically called the backlog. Read up on it. Use it. Stand by it and put any out-of-scope requests inside.

Once you have delivered a product on time that meets or exceeds base expectations, you can start to make it better. Continue to miss deadlines because of scope creep, and you will soon descend from *thrilling* to *meets expectations* to simply *get this done already*. Ever been on a winning project that sunk that low? I didn't think so.

SETTING UP A TEAM

What does the ideal mobile project team look like? Who should be on it, and what is left to be done? Great questions!

The first answer – it depends on your content path. You may need more or fewer subject matter experts (SMEs) depending on the state and depth of your content. You may need to lean heavily on your IT department if your solution touches a lot of outside services or servers, or if you have no internal developers that are ready to make the jump to mobile.

You just need to create the best, smallest team you can to make this happen. Nothing is worse than a big, unmanageable team with little overall direction. If team members are not connected to the project goals, then they will be less involved, less invested, less productive, and less valuable to the overall team. This is not where you want to be.

I believe that the team for a great mobile learning pilot or small-scale effort is comprised of the following people (we'll dive into their roles after this, and we'll also cover external stakeholders at that time):

- A content SME;

- A project manager/business partner;

- An instructional designer who has some familiarity with user interface/experience design;

- A mobile user interface design specialist;

- A mobile software developer/engineer;

- A Web developer for CMS or back-end development (if needed); and

- A tester/QA specialist.

That's it – six or seven people. You may want to know how so few people could create something of any scale. The key word here is scale. Let's not forget: A mobile app or website is meant to be focused, tailored, curated. Build the best and leave out the rest. You want people who can contribute meaningfully at every step, and you don't want to over-build. If I were to scale past a team this size, it would likely only be to add one or two more developers to work on technical components or functional subcomponents. Remember, this is not a space shuttle we are building here. This is a discrete piece of content that is created ideally to serve a single purpose well, not to serve many purposes in a mediocre fashion.

You may notice that we have merged a few roles and expectations. In mobile, a cross-functional team is a necessity. After all, we are striving for agility. We'll cover more of that in Chapter 12.

We would be talking about a large application – likely part of a comprehensive strategic effort – if the team were much bigger than this. Even apart from an undertaking of that size, a bigger team can sometimes be needed, especially if the work is complex or if the testing end of the project is involved. The key takeaway should be that in order to build light, compact learning experiences with any sort of velocity, you do not want to have a large structure of people and resources. You should have the people that you need to succeed. No more, no less.

Contrast this with an eLearning project where your team may look like this:

- A project manager;

- A business partner;

- An instructional designer;

- A user interface design specialist;

- A rapid eLearning software developer;

- A Flash developer for rich interaction creation;

- LMS developer;

- A functional tester/QA specialist; and

- A usability test specialist.

That looks a bit different, doesn't it? Remember, we're aiming to simplify. Step back from the edge. Stop inviting dozens of people to your meetings and just get the job done.

MAINTAINING VELOCITY AND MEETING DEADLINES

Velocity is a novelty when thought of as a project vector, but it is a real force you must consider. A project with continuous energy from kickoff to launch has a high percentage of pleased stakeholders and users. "We are the makers of music; we are the dreamers of dreams," after all. If we maintain velocity throughout the project, then we have a better chance of others coming along for the ride. We are more likely to discuss the content and concept with others. We will be less likely to see our project slowed by external stakeholders.

How do we do this? How can we prevent our project from turning into a bureaucratic mess – something mired in process and approvals, unable to move? Ironically, I believe that the real way to do this is through regular, consistent check-ins. Have a weekly meeting. Keep it short. Invite only those who add value and contribute. Use an online project-tracking tool that allows everyone to see the progress made that day or week. You are trying to set the stage for success. You have a far greater chance of achieving that by keeping people in the loop and making sure that obstacles are dealt with quickly. Keep your problems small and your decisions smaller, then you have something.

Don't let more than a day or two go by without your project manager talking to your designers or developers. Don't let your client-facing or business-partner-facing team member go more than a working week without touching base with the project manager. This doesn't need to be and shouldn't be happening. Make sure that everyone understands the work that was just accomplished, the work immediately in front of the team, and the issues the team is facing that might prevent it from achieving the project goals. These types of quick interactions across the entire group are the basic building blocks of agile development.

Velocity has little to do with the software you use, the development platform you have or the tools your developers are using to write code. The key is that through constant, small updates and check-ins, you are going to have a better handle on the work going through your pipeline. The quicker you are aware of issues in your workflow, the quicker you can respond to them. The faster you respond to them, the smaller the issues will be when you respond, and the easier it will be to deal with them.

ON RAPID DEVELOPMENT

You may already be a rapid software tool user. If you currently develop eLearning, chances are you have one or more of these products in your current applications directory. You may use them to build simulations, scenarios, or full-blown eLearning. Most rapid-development tools have a form of specialization or operation at which they excel, so it's not uncommon for someone to have and use two or three of these products.

These are called rapid development tools because they provide relative ease of use to developers. You don't need to write a lot of actual programming code in order to get a functioning piece of learning product completed. In my experience, this is often done by sacrificing reuse and modularity. Since mobile computing is such a fragmented landscape, this can cause problems. Rapid tools depend on the uniformity of the delivery platform. Today's mobile platforms are based on *custom* user experiences and features. Do not overestimate the importance of this.

Another shortcoming in the use of rapid tools is that the actual development process is anything but rapid. Constant revisions usually occur over the course of a rapidly created eLearning module. I believe this to be a symptom of a design problem typical of other digital media as well. This problem stems from the ease of development, allowing developers to make quick, often unplanned or poorly planned design decisions then compounding it by sharing those mistakes with external stakeholders. The result: Many revision cycles are required in order to correct everything. This over-sharing and over-developing allows people to focus on inappropriate aspects of a product at the wrong time. Too much detail and polish early on in the process front-loads the effort and backlogs the content-approval process. This can lead to elongated project deadlines and missed requirements.

I'm sure that rapid tool developers did not intend this at all. The tools were made easier to use in order to put the power of creation into the hands of the people who understand content and learning development. Unfortunately, in many ways, they have made instructional designers slaves to their design tools. The ease of the development should not take precedence over your methods. Use progressively more detailed deliverables in your creation process to keep your stakeholders focused on the key approvals they need to make at each step to keep the project moving.

While graphic user interface design is fun to unveil, it can also be one of the more expensive aspects to produce if you don't do it correctly. You should stay focused. Design the user interface (UI) and information architecture (IA) only after you have the learning objectives and content for the project. Anything sooner than that and you are likely to set yourself up for more revision cycles in the long run.

The Agile Release Cycle

Spend a little time considering mobile as an opportunity to make adjustments to your development process. Many of you are likely used to working in a fully waterfall or ADDIE type of development model. By adding wireframing and prototyping to the design phase of the project, you are already paving the way for a more modern, less expensive form of development: agile development.

If you have heard of agile development but haven't explored it, let me give you a brief overview of the process. Please don't take this as an exhaustive survey of the discipline. There have been volumes written on the subject, and there are many blogs and websites devoted to helping get up to speed with agile. This is information from the community at large and a list of core tenets.

The Agile Manifesto reads, in its entirety, as follows:

> We are uncovering better ways of developing software by doing it and helping others do it. Through this work we have come to value:
>
> **Individuals and interactions** over processes and tools.
>
> **Working software** over comprehensive documentation.
>
> **Customer collaboration** over contract negotiation.
>
> **Responding to change** over following a plan.
>
> That is, while there is value in the items on the right, we value the items on the left more. (Manifesto, 2001).

The real focus in agile development is to work iteratively, always striving to improve your work in incremental ways and using evolutionary steps to do this. You should always be ready to release with minimal prep time, and never leave your work in an unfinished, unstable state when copying back to a safe source or repository. This prevents errors from getting into the product and makes testing more streamlined.

Development work is typically split into time-boxed chunks, also known as "iterations" or "sprints." These sprints have basic goals set prior to commencing them so that the team knows what is expected in terms of key-feature groupings. As development progresses and these features are implemented, detailed design documents will emerge with the work. This is probably less predictive and rigid than your current process. This requires close collaboration, with colocated developers typically being close to each other in open working environments. With distributed teams, these obstacles can be overcome via collaboration tools like chat, IRC or message boards. Trust, accountability and autonomy are considered key values you should be fostering in these teams.

Beyond those basic concepts, keep in mind also that agile teams are typically cross-functional. This allows flexibility in picking up tasks and work responsibilities as needed to make deadlines during a sprint. Usually there is a lead developer or architect who manages client expectations, placing the client's desires into the planned workflow as sprint elements. This gatekeeper is responsible for keeping the sprints focused and on schedule.

ON AGILE DEVELOPMENT METHODOLOGIES

Agile is meant to be adaptive and flexible. While the designers and developers know in great detail what they will be working on for the next day or two, they may only have an idea of a few basic-feature sets they will be handling for the next week or month. It is probably that beyond the current sprint or iteration, the team will only have a basic overview or roadmap for future releases. This restriction in time and feature set allows agile to excel at preventing scope creep. The basic premise is that you can't get more work done if you don't have more time available.

I know that this sort of methodology is different than the formal processes that most learning-development teams employ. You must be able to weigh the pros and cons of these different approaches and realize that for certain projects different methodologies may yield better results. Your development process may need to change as your tools, goals and outcomes do as well.

If you have not spent much time considering the development phase milestones in your current development because it's not necessary, then I would ask that you do this at least in the mobile world prior to your first project. I tend to use the following major milestones as typical iteration points in small- to medium-sized efforts (under 500 hours, for example). These milestones are: Alpha, Beta and Release Candidate. Each of these milestones has a set of key questions, expectations, activities and deliverables in them that you will need to complete, test and prove.

Alpha

The Alpha phase is typically the first functional application build that you share with a circle of people outside the development team. This application may not yet be 100-percent functional. There may be content or media missing, or there might even be a few minor known bugs or issues in the build that need to be addressed.

The goals you are attempting to achieve in this build are twofold.

For the development team, you are primarily concerned with setting up the application's basic structure. This could be the various UI states or views. There will be a considerable amount of developer testing on the internal-application structure and data architecture. The developer's testing and goals of this phase will be concerned with choosing, building and testing the proposed application-development approach. Validation of the work done thus far and confirmation that work that is yet to be done will be possible are keys to the success of this phase.

The user testing of the Alpha is focused on basic application functionality, confined to the areas of the application that are completed and cleared for testing. Basic features should be verified as implemented and working. The overall user interface should be appraised and evaluated. Several groups also put basic usability tests into this phase, but in most cases this is better suited to Beta phase testing due to misunderstandings that can occur when content and features are missing.

The deliverable for this phase should be an Alpha build launchable under the same basic set of constraints that the final application will be used. Distribution of the Alpha may vary from how the actual product will be delivered.

Beta

The Beta phase expands on the Alpha. At this point, the content should be complete if possible. While there may be a few approvals or other gatekeepers who need to weigh in on the content for final approval, there is really no excuse for using unintended or placeholder content at this time.

The product should be functionally complete at this stage. Every major piece of functionality planned for the final release should be included and made available for review. Feature completeness aside, there may be many issues with this build from a production-quality standpoint. It is likely not fully optimized or performant, needing testing and improvements in these areas.

Often this may be the first build of the application or website available to a wider group of users in order to get feedback and aid with bug testing.

This product-release phase will probably not be distributed using the same mechanism that the final release will use. The deliverable is an installable or usable build made accessible to a selected group of testers.

Release Candidate

The Release Candidate is the last major phase of the product's development prior to its launch. Building on the work done in the previous phases, this functional and feature-complete build should incorporate the needed fixes identified in the last round of testing. Optimizations and performance testing should be incorporated here as well.

No new features or content should be added in this build that were absent from the previous build. If this build is found to be error free and performing, then it is ready to go to the release phase and be delivered. There are always errors in the software or product, so this concept of error-free is usually relegated to application blocks or crashes.

This product should be delivered using an instrument that is as close to a production-type mechanism as possible in order to test that portion of the product as well.

These phases may require adjustment in order to integrate them into your daily work. If you are interested in learning more about the process and agile development, I have added a few books in the reading list in the appendix of this book.

IN SUMMARY

With your content strategy under way, you are going to need to begin planning and development. There are a number of considerations to make in order to ensure success. Take the time here to prevent wasted effort in the future, using these steps:

- Establish a budget and schedules;

- Establish scope;

- Set up a team;

- Maintain velocity and meet deadlines; and

- Get ready to learn new development methodologies.

The budget may be out of your control, but when you contextualize it with the schedule and scope, you should be able to envision a solution and assemble a team that will execute that vision with clarity and success.

Any mobile project will need to have high velocity and not get mired in bureaucracy if you are to meet your schedule deadlines and stay within scope. Use your timeline as a measuring stick and make sure that you stay true to your launch date in order to judiciously prevent scope creep. Do this via careful up-front planning, limiting external stakeholders from obtaining late access to the project, and always saying "no" before agreeing to add any new features.

When moving from rapid eLearning development to a more software development-minded approach, you will likely need to shift your process and try various new methodologies. Don't shy away from them. You'll likely enjoy the freedom and capabilities these new tools afford you. Don't try to bring your old habits along for the ride just because they are familiar to you. You will not be pleased with the results.

ELEVEN

DESIGN AND DEVELOPMENT

MOBILE APPS VS. WEB APPS

You've probably debated this one with a team member or two. "We need an app." "No, a mobile website would be better." If you are like me, then you may have tired of this discussion by now and only answer when asked. You may be sitting back and watching the fireworks while the situation plays out in front of you.

The interesting part is that in the grand scheme, this discussion doesn't really matter. In the short term, decisions like this are tactical and need to be decided, but in the long view of mobile design, development tools, and device capabilities, there is little doubt that convergence is occurring and will continue to do so.

Before I explain that, let's establish a few basic rules of thumb regarding why you may want to consider a mobile website or mobile Web application (Web app) versus a dedicated mobile application, otherwise known as a native app or an app.

A mobile website and a mobile Web application are two terms used interchangeably that refer to one object: a Web-accessible piece of content or functionality that you can use on your Web-enabled mobile device. This content typically has a mobile-optimized user interface, uses basic mobile-optimized images and media assets, and leverages certain affordances or input methods that the device offers. These may be features such as basic hardware acceleration for CSS3, use of geolocation and basic accelerometer data, or perhaps the multitouch input capabilities of the screen. These mobile websites or apps are not delivered via app stores or marketplaces and are usually available for cross-platform use. They are typically written in JavaScript, which is an uncompiled, loosely typed programming language. The content is usually delivered in HTML5 specification markup, although XHTML is sometimes used. The content is styled via CSS (typically CSS3). This technology layer in a mobile Web application is most often referred to as HTML5. The goals for developing this way typically are the ability to access this content from many different devices and reduced maintenance due to fewer development requirements.

If you compare mobile websites with a dedicated mobile application or native app, you will notice key differences. Dedicated mobile apps are ultimately compiled. This means the assets, programming logic and any other resources needed for the application are fed through a translator that converts these assets into a highly optimized format known as bytecode. This bytecode is tuned for a platform-specific interpreting engine in order to ensure proper playback. This is typically done to take advantage of device-specific features and media capabilities. The more advanced media characteristics could be 3D graphics, sound synthesis, voice input, and much more – the list continues to grow with each successive OS version and the introduction of new devices. These apps can be developed using a number of languages, including JavaScript, but they are turned into a binary file that contains an associated package of assets, programmatic logic and other metadata required for functionality.

ON PLATFORMS AND OPERATING SYSTEMS

If your business is anything like most, then your organization probably houses a variety of mobile devices being used. With many different device form factors and capabilities spread across your workgroups, departments and business units, it's a challenge to keep up. Every time a new device or OS update is announced, there are cheers from your work force but a collective groan from the technologists required to support these new devices.

You understand why. We love each shiny new device and its cool features and eagerly look to use it when it becomes available. We are enamored with its capabilities and see no real downside. Then reality hits. We have to support yet another device or form factor inside of our IT organization/learning community.

Supporting a new mobile device is no small feat. Is the device secure? Will it perform well enough? Will it drain our resources? Will it put our information at risk? Keep in mind that at the present, this cycle of questions happens every three to four months.

Do you really want to answer that series of questions every quarter? I don't think so.

What we need is to put a plan in place that allows you to react to the marketplace in a predictable fashion. When the newest device hits, you don't shrink away from it – you embrace it, because you know you have laid the groundwork for how these events are handled.

Easier said than done, I know. There are several simple building blocks you can put into place to ensure you are ready for these inevitabilities:

- Discuss and write a bring-your-own-device (BYOD) policy. The actual stance of this procedure will vary according to your organization's needs, but whether you allow personal devices on your network or not is an issue you will continue to have unless you put it in writing.

- Choose an MDM/MAM provider. You need a way to publish apps, services and other information such as security profiles to these devices. Trying to do this on an ad hoc basis is a recipe for disaster. Maintenance, security and platform fragmentation will ultimately eat you alive without this step.

- Create an acceptable-use policy. What can your learners do on your network? What sites, services and apps are they allowed to use with company resources? What activities are they not allowed to engage in? When are they able to use these devices and services? This discussion will need to involve your legal team.

- Standardize your development team around one or two sets of tools. Make sure one of those is a cross-platform-capable tool that is built on documented and open standards in order to avoid vendor lock in. Get as good as you can at those. Either choose to ignore the others, or hire an external expert to assist with development outside your comfort zone.

- Task a specialist in your group with tracking trends, as well as major device and OS version releases. This doesn't have to be a full-time job, but it can take 30-60 minutes spread out over the course of a week reading mobile industry news sites, Twitter feeds and blogs to help you with long-term planning. Require this specialist to provide regular and timely updates to the people responsible for buying decisions.

- Download and update your apps and websites with beta versions of the latest mobile SDKs and OSs as they are announced and released. These SDKs and beta OSs are published by the vendors so that you can get up to speed with them and not have compatibility issues when they and the new devices that accompany them are finally released to the public. This is in stark contrast to past technology approaches where systems groups were reluctant to download and try out beta software of any kind. The speed to market wins again.

By placing tasks like these in your daily work flow and team processes, you are taking the steps needed to protect your investment in mobile.

Change is uncontrollable in this area. New devices and OSs are going to keep coming. New innovations in user interfaces and capabilities are only going to multiply. Sticking your head in the sand and refusing to adapt might have worked for you in the desktop/laptop technology world, but rest assured, that will not fly in mobile. Mobile is already on the same level as the consumer. The technology price point is low, and the devices are perceived as easy and fun. The timelines for product releases are faster than you can respond to with any sort of seriousness. Battling it out here is not advised. Go with the flow and redirect the discussion toward something productive.

USER EXPERIENCE AND USER INTERFACE

If you are coming to mobile learning from eLearning or other forms of learning content development, such as blended learning or instructor-led training, the concepts you have regarding user interface design and user experience are different from typical functional designers such as application designers, rich internet application (RIA) designers, and Web designers.

Instructional design is different from functional design, or graphical user interface design, and certainly different from user experience design. In one discipline, instructional design, the goal is to create an effective conduit for transferring knowledge. The other disciplines are centered on creating effective methods or mechanisms for accessing features and functionality. With one of mobile learning's primary goals being the delivery of information via rich features and functionality in a mobile form factor, you can see where this distinction trips up many people.

On one hand, you have ISDs who are used to providing instructional materials through interfaces that promote discovery and simulation-based interfaces. On the other hand, this information is being delivered on devices that are made to provide information with as little friction as possible. You can quickly see where the disconnect occurs. The concept that an interface needs to make someone think (i.e., many instructional designers' and eLearning user interface designers' approach to user interface design) is different than an interface that is designed to eliminate as much of that as possible (i.e., mobile Web and mobile app designers). In most websites and applications, any navigation or user interface that encourages the user to explore in order to learn how to use it is considered a failure, not an innovation. Don't make this mistake when moving to mobile. This new approach is about providing content quickly with as little clutter as possible. Investigation, exploration and curiosity are often considered strengths in many eLearning circles. This is not the case with mobile learning.

Your job is to adapt to this new approach. Users are not going to change their expectations for mobile. You must grow familiar with mobile design patterns and practices and begin to incorporate them into your creations on these new platforms. Users will not tolerate difficult-to-use or cutesy applications. They want their content or data now. Expecting your users to learn how your software works via a heuristic hunt-and-peck or mystery-meat approach is no longer acceptable.

There are minor exceptions to this rule using the concept of skeuomorphic designs. The term "skeuomorphic" means designing a derivative object that retains ornamental design cues to a structure that was necessary in the original, but is no longer needed in the new medium or delivery form. What is this, you ask? You see this every time you look at a digital slot machine that has rotating tumblers on a video monitor, observe someone smoking an electronic cigarette that looks like a real one, or walk down a street and observe windows on new homes with nonfunctional, unnecessary panes.

In the application design and development world, this design is prevalent in the media creation tools like audio and video editing suites where we use software that has dials and sliders that mimic the real world hardware we've moved away from. In the mobile world, this has become a bit of a cute nod to the particular device that an app or tool replaces – e.g., a compass, a barometer or a level. Do not attempt this without understanding what you are getting into. Critics are brutal.

You will need to become comfortable with the interface standards and guidelines for the delivery platforms you are targeting. You do know the platforms you are targeting, right? Just checking. If this has escaped you, be sure to go back and read Chapter 2 again.

Apple, Research in Motion (RIM) and Google have all published extensive documentation on what you should and shouldn't do when creating Web and app experiences for their respective platforms. As you sketch out and create wireframes for these applications, you would benefit from familiarizing yourself with these guides enough that you can envision the actual user interface elements you will use in the final implementation. Ultimately, you want to become familiar enough with the UI design controls, packages, and common patterns used for each platform that you can converse intelligently with your fellow designers. This fluency in the design language for mobile is just as important as understanding the proper assessment interactions for achieving learning goals. We are trying to provide the most usable interface we can to our learners.

WIREFRAMES AND PROTOTYPES

Many of you may be producing storyboards of your learning projects as you move from the instructional design phase to the graphic design or graphic user interface design phase. In application design, Web design, and now mobile user interface design, there is a similar yet distinctive design deliverable that you should begin to use as an assistant to move through complex design decisions prior to putting pixel to screen in a detailed design document.

This document is known as a "wireframe." The wireframe is a planning document created to help you diagram and relay key information architecture and an application's functional design treatments to a client and your development staff. The diagrams should be simple and understandable but detailed enough that a UI designer can take them and create a formal design mock-up along with existing client branding guidelines. A wireframe is typically produced after a list of functional requirements has been drafted, and a collection of use cases has been created. These initial documents help to inform the contents and approach of the wireframe.

A wireframe is more of an engineering document than it is an artistic document, with the emphasis on completeness and accuracy rather than artfulness. We are trying to provide a solid foundation of the types and volume of information we are providing in the product. We want the viewer of the wireframe to have a good idea of how the application will be navigated. Menus and tabs in all their varieties should be explained in detail, with real content used wherever possible. Design hierarchy and emphasis are explored here as well. The spotlight should be on focal points and calls to action, not the graphic design of the elements themselves. This distinction is subtle but vital to understand in order to leverage the wireframes' strengths.

Depending on your team and the skill sets contained in it, the role of the person who produces the wireframe may vary. Some teams have creative developers who can think innovatively and explore new paradigms in functionality. They manage this while grounding the work in their programmatic backgrounds, knowing that the approach they are suggesting is not only possible but is also the most logical one. Another team might have a cross-disciplinary designer with grounding in functional design and a penchant for making technically feasible approaches look beautiful. Whoever the person on your team is that produces these documents, remember this: Wireframes are to be used as both a thinking device for your internal team and an approval device to give your clients and/or stakeholders insight into the creative process at the appropriate juncture. Wireframes provide just the right amount of detail and help push the idea without being nearly as labor-intensive as producing a full mock-up. Use a pixel-perfect tool later for your formal mockups.

Let's take a look at a couple of wireframes and outline what makes them effective as both thinking devices and approval devices.

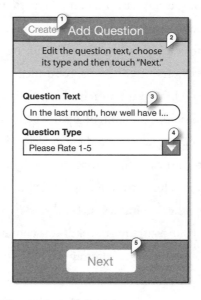

In the wireframe depicted here, it's easy to see the user is expected to input some information in the form fields on screen. There are a number of key navigational elements shown on the page as well.

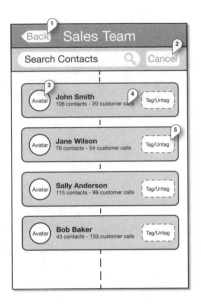

In the wireframe depicted here, you can see the user has the ability to filter, refine, and also adjust the current view via touch and gestures. The numbered call-outs on the page correspond to the tick marks shown in the screen design, giving more context and background information. These call-outs are necessary if we are to provide enough information to the developers on the project to set functional expectations. These call-outs also assist the client with seeing our true and full vision of the designer or developer.

Color and tone are commonly missing from these examples, but at this point those are not appropriate. Remember, we want the client to focus on what is really important at this time. We are not looking for feedback on the user interface from a purely graphic design perspective yet. The brand and familiar trappings of the user interface guidelines will come, as will the typeface, common logo, and imagery. We just don't want to spend time on this level of detail yet.

The real beauty of this approach is that we can take these wireframe designs and make them high-fidelity clickable prototypes in a short time. We'll cover that in the next chapter. For now, just trust that this is good. We need to determine concerns in terms of information architecture and usability before we waste precious cycles on polishing pixels and iconography.

USABILITY

Ah, usability! No other word strikes fear and loathing into the heart of a learning professional quite like it. Historically, learning professionals have found it challenging to excel in this area. There has always been a challenge in meeting usability expectations with our eLearning courseware. The problem stems from a lack of standards in design and implementation of a consistent and well-designed user interface.

Think about this. The average desktop application, even a custom one your organization designs and develops for in-house use, has a set of predefined user interface controls, widgets and design patterns that are generally expected. The scroll wheel, the drop-down picker, the tree-menu structure, the folder explorer – the list goes on, right? Even the custom-built applications your organization uses mostly implement reusable, standard, good ol' standby user interface elements. These apps also generally pass usability with little fanfare or issue.

Contrast this sharply to custom designed Internet applications and immersive experience websites with tons of custom user interface elements and divergent user experiences. The issues encountered in usability often skyrocket because of these.

Now, compare that same stumbling around to the average eLearning course and you may see a few correlations. The custom-designed exploratory navigation? *BONK!* Usability failure. The cool new menu and bookmarking metaphor you custom designed that one time? *BONK!* That was painful. See where I'm going here?

In mobile we have a responsibility to support those three use cases I mentioned earlier, taken from Josh Clark's *Tapworthy*: bored, local and microtasking (2010, p. 32). Not one of those use cases supports the users' experiences where the learners are so filled with wonderment about your content that they are willing to hunt and peck for the content they want or endure splash animations and noisy obstructions like in-line narration or obfuscated navigation to get to it. We need to get over ourselves and design a learning app that was meant to be used, not marveled at. How many times have you been congratulated on that whiz bang navigation you created for the course you just deployed? Maybe once. That was back in 2003.

Mobile application developers have a wealth of best practice information on UI design. As a learning designer getting into mobile, you should seek them out and read them. All major platforms have a basic set of guidelines available. For Apple's iOS, it's known as the Human Interface Guidelines or HIG for short. Google Android has a set of recommendations as well. So do BlackBerry and Windows Phone 7. If you are not looking over these standards before designing your experience, you will be doomed to continue hating your usability testers even when you move to mobile.

The bottom line is: know what your users expect in a mobile experience and deliver it. Choose to circumvent their usability expectations and take a different tact only if you know you have a winner and only if you can prove it through empirical research.

NATIVE VS. CROSS-PLATFORM DEVELOPMENT

When beginning the development phase, you'll be faced with a decision that should be academic at this point. What tools should you use to create your content or application? Based on the overall goals of your project, you will know if you are producing an app for one platform or more than one. This answer, along with a couple of others, will tell you which software development kit (SDK) and development path to take in order to reach your market.

Each mobile platform has its own specific application development toolkit which includes the integrated development environment (IDE) that has been created by the OS owner/vendor to facilitate the creation of dedicated mobile apps for that device family. Apple has the iOS SDK and Xcode, Google has the Android SDK and Eclipse, BlackBerry has the QNX SDK and the Legacy BlackBerry SDK in Eclipse, Windows Phone has .Net for Windows Phone and Visual Studio, and so on.

These IDEs are tailor-made for building applications for their respective platforms alone. You cannot, for example, use an out-of-the-box Eclipse install to develop iPhone apps. IDEs are intended to output your program logic and visual assets as apps for their specific needs. These development environments are considered the usual way that most developers take their apps through the process, including outputting apps for an online store or other deployment mechanism.

The above information makes it seem as though you must redevelop the application from scratch for each deployment platform. This would require you to write custom code for iOS, Android and so on. While this could certainly be the way you go about doing this, it could become difficult to manage from a long-term perspective. Think about what writing separate code for each family of devices means:

- Increased development cost;

- Increased time frame;

- Increased redundancy of efforts;

- Increased resource management;

- Reduced flexibility of future output;

- Reduced manageability of the codebase; and

- Reduced scope due to compromises that will need to be made.

Most of these IDEs are pretty extensible, however, allowing for plug-ins and other modular extensions to be installed in order to modify or add new features to the environments. In this space, a large and growing number of cross-platform tools have emerged that help you get your content to your learners. Some of the more popular ones we see today are:

- PhoneGap – http://phonegap.com;

- Titanium – http://appcelerator.com;

- Adobe AIR – http://adobe.com;

- Rhodes – http://rhomobile.com/; and

- MoSync – http://www.mosync.com/.

Let's a take a detailed look at a few of these. Daniel Pfeiffer (2011), Float's senior developer, pulled this together for our blog. Scores on the tables range from 1 to 3.

Rhodes

Rhodes is a Ruby-based framework that allows you to build your application a very similar way to the way you'd build a Ruby application. It offers support for iPhone, Android, BlackBerry, Windows Mobile and Windows Phone 7.

Rhodes offers support for the model view controller architectural pattern, allowing you to efficiently separate the business logic from the interface and easily make changes to a view (even simply by updating the data structure). Rhodes gives you the starting points for a handful of different views and you can tweak the templates to fit your needs simply by updating the HTML. The Ruby gets compiled down into bytecode to be executed on the device and each view is presented on the given device's browser rendering engine.

Rhodes goes hand-in-hand with Rhomobile's RhoConnect. RhoConnect makes it easy to communicate with (just about) any data source. RhoConnect makes all the necessary data available locally on the device so your application doesn't have to worry about communicating with a server. RhoConnect handles all the synchronization – both down from the server and up from the device. One of its most unique features is its ability to take advantage of the "push" capabilities available on BlackBerry and iPhone. RhoConnect will push changes down from the server when they occur without the device having to check and pull the changes down. This ultimately results in fewer network requests and an app that is more gentle on the battery. In addition, because RhoConnect is built using key-value stores (an implementation of NoSQL), it can easily handle changes to the data structure on the fly. RhoConnect is available outside of the Rhodes framework and can be used in any application.

If you have Ruby developers in-house, or if your site is already built on the Ruby framework, mobile app development will not be too far a departure. It's worth noting that the version of Ruby that runs on the device is a stripped-down version. Rhomobile has not taken every Ruby gem and made it available for use on mobile. That being said, the project is entirely open-source and there's nothing stopping you from taking the leap and implementing the gem yourself.

Rhodes is primarily geared toward data-centric apps – tables and lists and forms. It is definitely more enterprise-focused. You can add JavaScript to your views to make them more interactive, but Rhodes itself is really only concerned with the presentation of data.

Rhodes claims to appear far faster than apps written with an underlying SDK. This may be partially true: much of the logic within Rhodes apps (building the HTML for the view, handling the data downloaded from the server, etc.) are all executed at byte level, making them very quick. However, the data is presented primarily using Web views (using native components such as tab bars when possible). So, while a Rhodes-based app may be able to handle data quickly, its interface will only be as fast as the HTML layout engine on the device.

Category	Score	Details
Device Compatibility	3	Supports most mobile platforms including iOS, Android and BlackBerry.
Native UI Components	1	It's easy to get some native-looking elements, but actually implementing the native elements takes extra effort.
Access of Device Features	3	http://docs.rhomobile.com/rhodes/device-caps
General Performance	2	Suffers from an occasional view flicker or white screen.
Community	2	Pretty active Google Group, but not a lot of activity on Twitter.
Documentation	1	The documentation, while existent, feels very disorganized.
Sample Code	2	Code samples embedded within documentation; good, clean samples, but good luck finding them.
Data Handling	3	Only cross-platform framework with full support for an MVC.
Animation	1	Really doesn't handle animation; need to use JavaScript for any animation.
View Handling	3	The MVC structure makes building/managing views a breeze.

Rhodes models itself after Ruby. It handles data quickly,
but presents it only as fast as the device can.

Titanium

Titanium by Appcelerator claims to take your hard-won Web skills and turn them into mobile app development skills. It features a JavaScript API that provides access to native UI elements. The magic in Titanium happens during runtime in its bridge between the JavaScript and the native SDK. The bridge reads your JavaScript and uses it to build views that have the same features and performance as an application written in that native language. Currently, Titanium supports iPhone and Android (with BlackBerry support in beta mode for paid subscribers).

Titanium provides fantastic support for native UI elements. It does exactly what it says it does: you write your view once in JavaScript and then Titanium takes care of building the UI, using the proper UI elements for each platform. Like Rhodes, Titanium has great support for loading in data from a remote server and building a native-looking view based on that data. You could easily get an application with four tabs each with their own table view of data set up in a matter of hours using Titanium.

Titanium takes the native UI incorporation a step further than Rhodes; Rhodes includes support for native UI elements such as tab bars and mapping, but it relies on using the Web view for custom views (although a developer could use a native extension to build this capability). Titanium, on the other hand, gives access to almost every native UI element with support for customizing the look. You could build an entire app within Titanium without ever having to leave their API.

If you read closely, you'll find that Titanium takes your JavaScript and makes an app that looks like it was written using native code. Your JavaScript is compiled to symbols and then the SDK compiler combines the symbols with the Titanium API. While much of the code is mapped to the native code (like the interface elements), there is still an interpreter that handles dynamic code.

Without complete control over how these elements work together, you'll occasionally find yourself searching for workarounds when parts of their SDK don't seem to work correctly. The inability to manage when objects are removed from memory occasionally leads to performance issues or even leaks. Sometimes a view may appear blank while it's loading, which can detract from the native feel. There are almost always ways to work around whatever problem you run into, but you may find yourself spending a lot of time trying to get your app from "really good" to "great."

Category	Score	Details
Device Compatibility	2	Works with Android 3.x and iOS. Support for BlackBerry in beta.
Native UI Components	3	Supports nearly every native device UI component.
Access of Device Features	3	Provides JavaScript abstraction for all the common features; includes some lower level network control.
General Performance	2	Occasionally suffers from blank views while loading.
Community	2	Active community (although a handful of questions go unanswered).
Documentation	3	Great API documentation.
Sample Code	3	The Kitchen Sink app is a great example of all the features of Titanium.
Data Handling	2	Easily parse through JSON and XML support is pretty good; easy to build views based on data.
Animation	2	Can animate most UI elements, but don't expect very advanced animations.
View Handling	3	Effortlessly manage and customize different views of the application; each window can have its own namespace.

Titanium features great support and sample code.
On occasion, not everything works perfectly.

MoSync

MoSync takes a different approach to cross-platform mobile development in that it tries to appeal to multiple audiences. It has its own SDK built with C/C++ that gives the developer access to many of the standard C libraries, graphic and media classes, the networking layer, native UI elements and more. In addition,

MoSync's Wormhole JavaScript Library allows JavaScript to utilize its C/C++ SDK. At this point, it offers support for Windows Mobile and Windows Phone 7, Symbian S70, Android, iOS and Moblin/MeeGo.

MoSync approaches the simulator differently. One of the rules of thumb of mobile development is always test on the device because you can't trust the emulator. MoSync approaches the problem differently with their emulator (MoRE). Instead of trying to replicate the device in the emulator, MoSync uses the emulator as the standard and tries to get each device match that standard. Furthermore, MoRE actually can read presets from a device profile database and emulate screen size, available memory, etc. In addition to using MoRE, you also have the option of using the native emulator/simulator for your target platform.

With the release of the HTML5 extension of its SDK, MoSync also introduced an improved mobile development workflow called Reload. Reload lets you work on your HTML5 app on your computer and see the results immediately on the device or simulator with the push of a button – no need to compile during development. As with any Web-based cross-platform solution, the app is eventually limited to what the HTML rendering engine and JavaScript engine are capable of doing. MoSync attempts to help you over this barrier by opening access to the native UI and entire C/C++ library through their JavaScript API.

The MoSync SDK (both the C/C++ and Wormhole JavaScript Library) is accompanied by decent documentation and very helpful Getting Started guides. In addition, members of the developer community are fairly helpful since they usually respond to questions within a day. MoSync offers numerous example applications (although most of them are very basic) to help you grasp the basics of the SDK.

Category	Score	Details
Device Compatibility	2	Doesn't have full support for BlackBerry; iPhone support is still limited in some regards.
Native UI Components	1	Only supports iPhone and Android; doesn't work in MoSync emulator.
Access of Device Features	1	Supports some lower level network control, but no support for accelerometer or camera in most phones.
General Performance	3	Runs smoothly; get a lot of control over how fonts are rendered to the screen.
Community	2	Has a growing community on both Twitter and forums.
Documentation	3	Lots of documentation about framework and an excellent API reference.
Sample Code	2	Provides a decent amount of sample code; could really benefit from an app like Titanium's Kitchen Sink.
Data Handling	1	Contains XML parsing libraries, but lacking support for JSON or other data formats.
Animation	2	There are plans to include support for OpenGL; because it's written in C, there is support for some drawing and simple physics libraries.
View Handling	1	Doesn't provide support for an MVC; requires a little extra effort to create views for data.

MoSync doesn't allow much access to the device's features, but apps built using the toolkit run smoothly.

PhoneGap

The community for PhoneGap is impressive. I'm not referring to size so much as I am referring to the rate of growth. In 2009, it featured 4,298 posts and more than doubled to 9,561 posts in 2010. In October 2011, Adobe announced its purchase of Nitobi, the parent company of PhoneGap. This is just a picture of the PhoneGap community and how fast it is growing. If you decide to jump into PhoneGap, there is a very vibrant community waiting to help you.

PhoneGap uses straight-up HTML, CSS and JavaScript. There is no interpretation of your code (this generally makes for less unexpected results on different platforms); PhoneGap literally loads your app into a chromeless Web browser. Further, the PhoneGap API runs on a very extensible plugin architecture. If PhoneGap doesn't already support the feature you need, you can easily write a plugin yourself (in fact, there's a good chance its already been written and is available for you to download).

Don't expect to write a Web app that works beautifully on your desktop browser and to be able to drop it onto your phone and have it run the same way...especially if you're trying to use Java Script-based animations. The HTML layout engine on mobile devices simply can't keep up with its desktop counterparts.

Furthermore, PhoneGap does nothing to emulate the native device UI (although, as always, there are plugins and customizations that bridge this gap a little bit). You could emulate the UI with HTML and CSS, but what we're finding is that a lot of people build their app for the iPhone, and then use the same UI on the Android. The bottom line is this: the iPhone UI makes no sense to an Android user. Don't do that.

Category	Score	Details
Device Compatibility	3	Supports most common OSs including iOS, Android and BlackBerry.
Native UI Components	0	No native UI support. There are forks that do offer some support, however.
Access of Device Features	3	JavaScript provides great abstraction class for all common device functionality.
General Performance	3	PhoneGap itself performs great; performance issues arise from poorly written apps and slow devices.
Community	3	Very vibrant community; lots of activity on forums, Twitter and blog articles.
Documentation	2	API reference has gotten a lot better; could still stand to clean up wiki.
Sample Code	2	Good sample code for PhoneGap API, but not a lot of support from PhoneGap for building good mobile apps. However, there are plenty of blog articles.
Data Handling	1	Left completely up to JavaScript and device's implementation.
Animation	1	CSS animation works great on iOS devices; leaves a lot to be desired elsewhere.
View Handling	0	Completely in the hands of the developer how the app is going to manage views.

PhoneGap offers no native UI components or view-handling ability,
Its community, however, is booming.

The first step in choosing a mobile cross-platform framework is determining the needs of your app. If you're looking to make an app that consumes a lot of data, take a look at Rhodes. If you're looking to take advantage of all the native UI elements, try out Titanium. If you're looking to build a custom interface that can take advantage of your Web development skills, take a look at PhoneGap or MoSync. These are definitely not hard and set rules – just guidelines to help you make an educated decision. It's also important to evaluate what skills you have - if you've never touched Ruby before in your life, Rhodes may not be the best direction.

In closing, here is a summary of each platform and whether it offers adequate support for a given area.

Category	Rhodes	Titanium	MoSync	PhoneGap
Device Compatibility	●	○	●	●
Native UI Components	○	●	○	○
Access of Device Features	●	●	○	●
General Performance	●	●	●	●
Community	●	●	○	●
Documentation	○	●	●	●
Sample Code	●	●	●	●
Data Handling	●	●	○	○
Animation	○	●	●	○
View Handling	●	●	○	○

A comparison of some of the major cross-platform development tools today

A few other cross-platform tools that may be worth evaluating for your needs are:

- Corona;

- MonoTouch and MonoForAndroid – http://xamarin.com/ monotouch, http://xamarin.com/monoforandroid; and

- Unity – http://unity3d.com.

Beyond those, there are interesting rapid app-creation tools coming out that look to be promising, but they are a bit early in their overall maturity level. For example, AppGyver and the MIT App Inventor tools for Android OS look promising in this space, but these tools are new and may not serve production needs for some time.

At this point, app development tools and techniques are developing a frontier – lots of untamed paths and little documentation for them. You definitely want to weigh issues like support, community, and documentation when it comes time to choose your software development tools. You don't want to make a choice that you will come to regret when you are halfway into your development phase or even worse, a few months after your app launches and the tools you have chosen are now orphaned, defunct, or swallowed up by a larger company with a different mission or agenda than that of the originators.

A unique way to think about this is to equate the choice to the addition of a team member for the project. Does the tool make your job easier? You want to know if it contributes or detracts and whether it speeds completion time or slows it. Is it dependable, or is it flaky and hard to read when it messes up? Read the documentation and verify there are good troubleshooting and debugging resources. Does the tool have good references or recommendations? Check the community for this. Has it been around for a while? You want a tool with maturity and longevity for this kind of production.

Let's move on. Once you have the development process underway, how do you test the work in progress?

TESTING & QUALITY ASSURANCE

You may believe you have a rigorous testing process in place if you have been building eLearning for a while. This may be true. I will caution you, though: Nothing in eLearning is as involved as testing even a mild application with a cross-platform delivery target. When you add in mixed connectivity environments and alternate device factors like tablets, you have a much bigger job on your hands than you ever did with eLearning.

Consider this scenario in eLearning. You probably have a set operating system, browser version, and a plugin version for your desired runtime player – (be it Flash, Windows Media, QuickTime or other) – in your IT landscape. Users were expected to connect to the LMS via a work-provided desktop or laptop computer that had an identical hardware configuration as 90 percent of the population. You could guarantee the bandwidth requirements and even screen resolution. The users' context in accessing the content was uniform across all the learning content you delivered.

In the mobile learning world, virtually none of that is constant. We've already talked about the ever increasing number of devices, so you can probably see how that adds to the complexity. Beyond that differences in your users' tech knowledge, the variations in connectivity quality and speed, and social and physical settings dramatically complicate the situation.

Most mobile websites or apps connect to databases, content-management systems, or knowledge bases. If you primarily made self contained learning modules that had no communication with other servers except through the LMS via a simple JavaScript program, then you might be unfamiliar with this avenue of testing.

You are going to need a test plan to get you through this phase. In producing this plan, a few of the documents you have already created will help you. Observe again the user personas, use cases, storyboards and/or wireframes as well. These documents provide a blueprint of how your application will function. Use these documents to provide the set of desired actions and outcomes for the effort you are creating. Be exhaustive in your research and collation. Go through these narratives and screen sketches obsessively, giving each screen a defined name (if it doesn't have one after) and do the same for all the elements on every screen. I recommend creating a naming convention for your mobile projects to serve as a reusable framework that will make this easier the next time around. Place these named elements in the first column of a spreadsheet as the label for each row. The other columns across the top should be labeled with the test OS and device used, the user interaction used to trigger or enable the element, the desired outcome, and the test case name you assign to it.

Element	Test Case Name	OS	Device	Trigger	Desired Outcome	Actual Outcome	Pass/Fail
Main Menu	V1_tc01	iOS 5.1	iPad	Touch	Display main menu	Display main menu	Pass
Share Button	V1_tc01	iOS 5.1	iPad	Touch	Trigger action sheet	Crash application	Fail
Contacts Button	V1_tc01	iOS 5.1	iPad	Touch	Display contacts list	Display contacts list	Pass
Favorites Button	V1_tc01	iOS 5.1	iPad	Touch	Display favorites list	Display favorites list	Pass
Locations Button	V1_tc01	iOS 5.1	iPad	Touch	Display locations	No actions occured	Fail

Sample test case spreadsheet format

These do not make up everything that will need to be tested, but test cases will give you a list that is unique to your application. There are also many other boilerplate test items that you will want to include.

These items will vary from one organization to another due to expectations from external stakeholders such as IT, branding and marketing, legal, and any other group that typically has input in the testing process. Some examples you may want to try:

- What happens when the app's Internet connection gets severed?

- What happens when the device goes to sleep?

- What happens when the user puts the device into lock mode?

- What happens when the device is set to airplane mode?

- What happens when the user rotates the device?

You see where I am going with this. The goal would be to set several basic expectations for how any websites or apps function when they are released by your department.

After the testing plan is created, it's time to test! You'll need a set of test mobile devices and also a logging tool. This will allow you to both note the issues that you find and also assign these issues to a staff member to complete the necessary fixes. I highly recommend moving your testing and issue-logging process to an online project management tool if you haven't already. You want the most recent information available to all the team members involved. This could be a dedicated tool such as FogBugz or Assembla, but even a Google Docs spreadsheet or Google Base database would be better than the unconnected alternatives you may have been using for smaller testing processes. Don't even think about using a flat text file or similar document that has to be updated on an internal server or sent to the project lead via emails. That is a recipe for information loss.

Some key items you will want to store in the issue-logging tool (these may vary based on your needs, but this is a good start):

- Issue Title – Make this descriptive, but short (e.g., "The Title on the Entry Detail Screen Is Incorrect");

- Issue Description – A slightly longer narrative description, perhaps with a proposed resolution or desired outcome (e.g., "The title currently says 'Entry Detail View' but should actually contain the entry's real name, not placeholder text.");

- Affected Platform(s) – List the delivery platforms you are testing on, preferably with OS version listed;

- Found in Build Version – Could be a release number (e.g., 0.9.1) or name (e.g., "Alpha," "Beta," etc.);

- Fixed in Build Version – You want to track this as well to measure progress and find out if any regression issues occur;

- Date Logged;

- Date Fixed;

- Date Due – If you can't give a due date for when you need it fixed, how can you expect anyone to make it a priority?;

- Reported by – Most issue systems log this automatically, but if not, this is a handy field to have;

- Assigned to – Should be a list of the person(s) who should be testing or working on this issue;

- Priority – I've seen this done as a ranking from 1-5, Low to High, and also as a series of qualitative adjectives such as trivial, minor, major, block and crash. I prefer Low to High, personally;

- Steps to Replicate – This isn't used that often as a field, but when it is, it's helpful. The easiest way to fix a defect for most developers is to see it. The steps to replicate an issue allow them to do just that. If your system doesn't support a field like this, consider adding this copy to the issue's description field;

- Attachments – These could be screenshots of the issue occurring, or a media asset like a photo, piece of copy or video that you can use to produce the issue. In lieu of having a proper list of steps to replicate, this can be used as an aid for the developer;

- Related Test Case – If you have named and organized test cases prior to testing, you can use these named tests as references to assist with the steps to replicate and also determine whether any regression issues are occurring; and

- Console Messages – If you have debugging turned on and the user can provide you detailed console reports from the application (you may want to provide them assistance to do this), you will often find that you can spot the issue without having to test the software to replicate it yourself. These logs may look like gibberish to mere mortals, but they can be powerful support documents to a seasoned developer.

Your list may be slightly bigger or smaller than that, but in order to have a streamlined, usable testing process that assists in providing quality to the overall product, it should not have fewer details.

After the issue is logged, the development staff member will make the required fixes, integrate them into the next build of the project, and reassign the ticket to the testing team. The testing team should review the issue in the provided build and mark the issue as resolved if it is so. If not, reassign the problem to the development team and have them try again. Hopefully this will be a rarity.

I'm going to talk more about deployment and releases in Chapter 13, so if I didn't cover your questions here, just wait.

IN SUMMARY

As you begin your design and development phases, you must learn about a number of topics that will dramatically influence your path.

You will need to review the business case to determine whether or not you really need to commit to building an app. This isn't a tough decision unless you let it become one. You should begin any project with an understanding of the technology platform that will be used by learners for this content. These decisions will factor in on the choice of tools and processes you will use to produce your work.

Don't stray too far from the norms for your platform when designing the user interface and user experience. Making your learner work to use your app, website or service is a surefire way to start off on the wrong foot.

While native development tools are always great to use, sometimes budget constraints will dictate the use of a cross-platform tool. Remember that there are always compromises you will make when you opt for a path like this. Choose your tools wisely, because they are not created equally.

If you come from an eLearning background, then testing and development workflow in mobile will be different than what you may find familiar. Use rigor and create a replicable testing process to ensure quality. Consider using agile development in order to keep scope creep to a minimum and maintain your overall release schedule.

ON PROTOTYPES
AND PILOTS

WHEN TO PROTOTYPE

Prototyping may be a lost art in the learning and development world. Rapid tools for eLearning may have dulled our skills in building something quick to test or get an idea to a few testers for quick feedback. For years prototypes haven't been needed because rapid-development tools make it so easy to bring instructional materials to our audience, especially when you have high-quality assets you can procure from marketing or shoot with your digital SLR or smartphone camera. We've been able to move from script to storyboard to final deliverable in such a short time that creating a prototype seems like an over-engineering exercise.

However, with recent changes in tooling and design, and a totally new interaction model offered by mobile, you may find yourself in foreign territory. Many of your existing eLearning tools may have deficiencies in the mobile area, or they don't function at all. It's not that bad. We have a number of options available for us in mobile development. Everything from low-fidelity paper prototypes to high-fidelity clickable prototypes can be options for bringing our ideas to our team and stakeholders.

When sketches and whiteboards are just not enough, you'll know you need to create a prototype. These are necessary when people need to experience your website or application in order to visualize how it will work and how they will integrate it into their workflows. You create a prototype to prove your concept and even to connect the systems represented in it. The connection points could be somewhat less than obvious depending on the integrations, with customer relationship data and sales bulletins intermingled with training content. Make clear what you are proposing at this stage.

You'll need to start a prototype phase in time to validate its results in advance of a formal development effort or a larger pilot project. You'll want to have resources available for both the prototype testing and the follow-up survey or measurement phase, where the results will be collated and the findings shared with the team at large.

This is harder than it sounds. All too often I have seen issues arise when a prototype testing phase ended and not enough time was given to analyze the results before jumping to conclusions. Just remember: a prototype without analysis and testing is a proof of concept, not a complete prototype. While that's not bad, it is not what we are looking for here.

HOW TO ENTER A PROTOTYPE PHASE

A prototype must be a deliberate undertaking. You will need a focus and a number of tests that you plan to run in the process. Your prototype may be design oriented, function oriented or perhaps a test for usability and user acceptance. Whatever your goals, it is key to establish them right away. A successful prototype is usually the first version of a product meant for testing purposes. It might not work as a program or unit, but it is made to present a potentially viable product visually. Depending on your project's needs and sometimes the culture of the company or the team assembling, this state of the application can vary in terms of detail.

At the outset there are a number of factors you need to be aware of and prepare for. To come out of the prototyping phase successfully, you must address the following in the initial planning stage:

• Prototype goals;

• Prototype fidelity;

• Prototype deliverable format;

• Prototype designer;

• Prototype developer; and

• Prototype content developer/writer.

The goals you set for your prototype will inform the other points listed above. A prototype that is created to prove the feasibility of a human/computer interaction or solve a usability issue obviously has different fidelity and design needs than one that tests and proves data communications with a server or between servers. You will need to make your goals explicit at the onset if there is any hope that you will be successful.

Prototype fidelity is a more abstract concept. To help, take a look at the graph below, mapping a prototype's trueness to its final deliverable (fidelity) against the effort level or scheduling it's going to take to get it done.

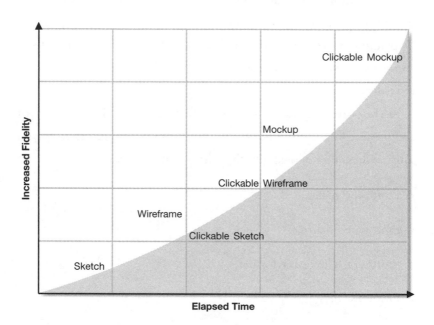

It boils down to this: The closer the prototype is to the expected final outcome, the more time and effort the prototype is going to take to produce. The interesting point here is that a clickable sketch, which takes little time to produce (relatively low fidelity from an image standpoint), may actually pass a important usability test or prove whether people will use an app or service. As you can guess, you can accomplish much without breaking the bank.

There are lots of great products that allow you to take design assets and move them directly into a prototyping phase with little (if any) programming requirements or extra work. Many of these tools are

Web-based and operate as software-as-a-service (SaaS), so their overall licensing requirements and costs are low. Daio, FieldTest and Justinmind's Prototyper are just three that spring to mind. Others have found great success with tools like Keynote and even PowerPoint when used for clickable, high-fidelity prototypes. Don't believe me? Check out keynotekungfu.com to see just how far you can take presentation software as a prototyping tool. There are options out there. You just need to be creative.

The deliverable format doesn't have to be a head-scratcher, either. You will need to get the prototype out to people and have them use and review it. That should be a baseline expectation. A prototype is not set up to succeed if it requires a special software install or a trip over to the testing lab in order to try it. Prototyping tools should be accessible and usable with a minimum fuss. This can be done efficiently over the Web with rapid-prototyping tools. You can even put the prototype at a hidden URL or password-protect it with one of the many aforementioned packages available today.

In order to maintain continuity, the designer and developer resources you use on the prototype should ideally be the same as the ones you will use to create the final application. If this is not possible due to time constraints or resourcing issues, you should make sure that the team that puts the prototype together is at least as skillful as the team that handles the final development. You cannot assume that a rookie team or junior staff member can execute a crucial step of this process as well as a senior level team member. Success is of the utmost importance in this phase, so the prototyping team must be staffed accordingly. If a junior staff member is the only one available to create the prototype, please have his or her work independently audited prior to wider circulation.

You should plan on having an available copywriter for the prototyping phase. A product that's going to your testers rife with typos and grammar issues or overflowing with placeholder or *lorem ipsum* text is doomed from the start. Be sure to put the proper amount of focus on the application's content. Delivering a polished prototype that the testers can relate to will pay off.

When you present the prototype to the testing team, have a form of standardized reporting in place that will allow you to receive consistent input from all team members. This could be an email form, survey or even a formal testing period with video recording and transcripts. However, understand that formality is no substitute for thoroughness and adherence to your original goals. Keep matters tightly focused, and you'll get the results you need to make informed decisions. Provide no standardized measurement framework, no timeline and no mechanism for feedback, and your prototype will be doomed to fail, no matter how pretty it is.

WHEN TO PILOT

You may have experience with pilot programs. Technology departments frequently use small-scale pilots to test out a product, methodology or new process early in the evaluation stages of a project. Learning teams may be familiar with pilots as well, but probably only for the bigger-picture items like rolling out a new major piece of curriculum or LMS.

Introducing mobile learning into your curriculum warrants such an approach. We need to know what's going to stick and what deliverables are best suited for your learners' needs. Beyond that, there are so many variables in terms of technology, connectivity, software and platforms that need to be determined that it makes sense to try out a smaller effort before committing a mass of funding and resources.

This seems like common sense, but without proper planning for a pilot, you will not be any further along in the decision-making process at the end of developing your pilot than you were before you set out on this path. You must be clear, concise and consistent in your pilot's overall goals, communications and rollout procedures.

You'll know you are ready to pilot a strategy and implementation path when you have more questions than can be answered by one or two prototypes. If your prototypes have been well-received, and you have a few items or areas of improvement that can be brought to a wider audience and possibly used in the actual day-to-day business, you may need a pilot. If your management is on board with allocating resources for the technology costs and design of a larger program, you may have the green light.

A pilot, by definition, is a test to determine feasibility, development time, approximate cost, planning for adverse effects, and evaluating the impact an effort could have on your work. It is created to improve on the design of your smaller efforts prior to the full rollout of a strategy. Pilots are frequently carried out before large-scale deployments to avoid wasted efforts and resources. A pilot study is handled best using a sample that represents as closely as possible the intended population of users. It often provides valuable insights and is highly recommended for testing out mobile learning projects following the initial prototyping phases.

The pilot should be as fully formed prior to development as possible. Changing direction during the middle of a pilot test will provide you with less useful information than a test that you allow to run its course. If you want to do something that allows your idea to grow and morph as the test progresses, consider starting a couple of smaller pilot efforts simultaneously and do a multivariate analysis instead. This will require a little legwork. You are in essence creating multiple prototypes – each with specific design or development paths and end-deliverables – and testing them simultaneously with alternate groups of testers. Test the results and effectiveness of the actual product use rather than the qualitative impressions of the users. Did one approach end up being more effective than another? If so, you have received the answer you needed.

COMPONENTS OF A SUCCESSFUL PILOT

As mentioned before, the pilot should be as true to final deployment as possible to test not only the idea and the approach to design and development, but also the logistics of the deployment. This is the key to getting an accurate sense of what the full effort will be to finally deploy your application.

All of the challenges, obstacles and opportunities should be identified during this small-scale rollout. We are attempting to see what floats and what sinks. A good pilot covers the entire lifecycle of your planned program.

This expansive type of pilot can be labor intensive. Ideally, it builds on what you learned from building a prototype or two. The products used then can be reused now, but don't trot out something your users have seen before. If you received valuable feedback from the prototype testers – say, for instance, that the user interface was tough to use, or the content was a bit drab – then use that feedback and fix those issues prior to the pilot rollout. Prototype testers who have become pilot testers will be able to see the progress you made, and the components of the pilot will show better during user acceptance and usability testing. Management will see increased involvement and improved metrics from the initial effort. Stakeholders will see the potential and have something to talk about.

The pilot's test features or even products are obviously a key component of the program. After all, what would you test if you had nothing to try? However, they won't be everything that needs to be examined. You are going to need a comprehensive approach if you are aiming for success. Consider each of the following points while crafting your pilot plans:

- Software platforms and requirements;

- Design and development practicalities;

- Branding and organization identity standards;

- Marketing and evangelization;

- Change management; and

- Deployment and measurement.

Execute these successfully and you will have a winner. Miss one or more at your own risk. You'll need to prioritize, but at this point, if it's a pilot of any substantial scale, then it's an idea or ideas that has been validated during the lead-up proof of concept or prototype stage that got you this far. The team may start to grow a bit here, as you'll possibly need to engage outside help in order to complete the secondary and tertiary goals of your pilot effort. Project management is also something you're going to need to watch closely as you move to pilot kickoff.

The components themselves have moving parts in each of them. Software and platforms are going to be a factor, because you go from a "what if we do this?" to a "when we do this" mentality. The platforms will matter because of the device profiles you may need to take into account.

The process for choosing tools needs to match up with the talent and technology profiles you may have in place. You can't build a large-scale mobile learning rollout with tools you don't already have or aren't willing to acquire and train your team to use. Who would build it? Who would maintain it? The pilot process should have a healthy dose of reality in terms of exploring the actual project's lifecycle. This includes updates and ongoing maintenance of the products and support system.

If your prototype project was small enough to stay off the radar of your branding and standards group, you got lucky. Anyone in learning and development knows that navigating these waters can be tricky. Adding any stakeholders to the mix can be a tough proposition, but when you are adding the sharpest, most creative people in your organization to your approval chain, you must come prepared with your A game. You'll need to have your assets and design deliverables in proper shape and make sure you have read the provided documentation.

Often, branding departments have training materials available for you to use. Sometimes these may even be eLearning or training content your team previously produced. Be sure you familiarize yourself with their courses. Mobile is a new area for many branding departments, so don't be surprised if there are several bumps along the way when your work comes under the scrutiny of these outside groups. Project an air of collaboration, acknowledge that we are all learning and new at this, then move on. A battle at this point is not worth it and may create an adversarial situation that will be tough to back down from. You are trying to build new alliances here, not rehash old conflicts or problems.

You are likely not the best at promoting your work. After all, you're a learning professional and not a marketer, right? You will need to add a new hat to your collection. No one is going to know just how great your new efforts are and what the business impacts are unless you let them know. You must be creative and relentless in promoting the new groundbreaking work you are doing. Let people know about the cool factor – the importance of it. Be sure to illustrate just how different the project is and how it is going to affect their day-to-day work in a positive way. This is change management wrapped in a shiny package. Build enthusiasm via newsletters or promo videos delivered via traditional company messaging platforms. This isn't your old learning promotion or letting people know about a new LMS or piece of courseware. This deserves proper focus. Be ready to answer questions. Have an FAQ ready. Prepare screen casts or annotated screenshots in advance. Have a blog post or two talking about key features and the benefits of what you are promoting. Use video interviews with a few of your prototype users espousing the usefulness of your earlier version. Use your wiki and internal social media platforms like Yammer to augment your messaging.

Finally, once your pilot is in full swing, don't forget to check in with the tools you have put in place to measure results. Do you have access to those tools? They may be LMS data points, Web analytics tools or perhaps even surveys. Be sure to provide reporting to your team on salient details or when progress has been made in order to continue to build interest, gain support and start building a case for your project. Reverse engineering a story out of statistics is tougher if you haven't been checking them on a regular basis, so don't let this get ahead of you. You want to make sure that when the pilot ends, you have some solid information that's ready to share. The last hitch you want to encounter is to let the energy die because you weren't thinking ahead, and the meeting you needed to relay these numbers to the management team slips to the next month. Be prepared to share.

IN SUMMARY

A prototype project may be a new experience for you as a learning creator. This may be for a number of reasons, but to test and identify key factors you're going to need in your larger effort, you should consider putting it on your radar when you move to mobile.

Be sure to have ample time to build a meaningful prototype that stakeholders can weigh in on. Remember to share your goals with the testers and the users of the prototype in order to lay out your expectations for their focus while trying it. Prototypes can have widely varying levels of fidelity and utility, so if you don't cover these with your testers, you may be setting yourself up for failure before they even give you feedback. Having your framework in place to accept and collect this feedback for review and processing is vital.

After a prototype project or two, you should consider running a pilot program to work out any kinks found across the entire product lifecycle. Everything from design to delivery to post-launch maintenance should be considered in a comprehensive pilot project.

THIRTEEN

DEPLOYMENT AND LIFECYCLE

LAUNCHING CONTENT

You've done it! Your website, SMS app or mobile application is ready to go. Now what? Push the button. No wait – Not that one!

You are probably like most people when it comes time to actually getting that first mobile effort out there. What next? How do we get this mobile website to our learners? If you are accustomed to living in the comfort of your shady LMS for any great length of time, then the path to publishing an mLearning product will be different. Everything was so simple back then (at least once you got the hang of it, right?). Mobile is fraught with perils and every turned corner reveals a new surprise. What fun!

Common issues that people grapple with as they begin the deployment phase for a mobile-optimized website are:

- Do we need to secure publicly accessible Internet or intranet space?

- Do we need to add custom meta tags to page templates?

- Do we need to set up a new companion Web page or website?

- Will the Web services layer you are using with the app stand up to the brunt of the user base?

- Do we need to re-prep all our media assets to go mobile?

- How will you make sure your website is secure and performing?

- Can analytics be put on a mobile site?

- Can the same JavaScript libraries that we used on the desktop version of the site be used for mobile devices?

- What is all this talk about responsive Web design, and how does it apply to my learning content?

Some of the questions I hear when people are moving to a mobile app are:

- How does all this code signing and provisioning work, anyway?

- How do we get our app ready for final publishing?

- What's with all these icon sizes and splash screen sizes?

- Does any of this metadata actually matter?

- What's the difference between development and distribution certificates?

- How can we get this app to our users without deploying it to an app store or other marketplace?

- Is my information in the app secure?

- Who makes the final build?

- Who submits the final build?

- How will I know how the application is coming along?

- How does the approval process work for apps in various app stores?

- How long does approval take?

- Can I remove an app after it's been launched?

- How often can I update an app in a store?

As you can see, regardless of the deployment path you are following, you are bound to hit a few stumbling blocks. Keep in mind that this is *not* rocket science. Even apps *about* rocket science don't require rocket science for deployment.

THE BASICS OF THE MOBILE WEB

The mobile Web seems like a strange land to many designers and developers who haven't already created their first mobile projects. While there are certainly more considerations to take into account due to device and user constraints, it's no more complicated than our first forays into the World Wide Web.

Several key tips to remember as you ready your content for the mobile Web:

- Use Web standards;

- Say goodbye to plugins;

- JavaScript is your new best friend;

- Try something new;

- Know your gesture and device inputs;

- Understand your hardware capabilities;

- Should we opt for backwards compatibility or progressive enhancement? What's the difference?

- Don't try to cram a desktop site into a mobile box;

- Consider mobile first; and

- Optimize, optimize, optimize.

A mobile website has a lot of dependencies. The Web browsers on mobile devices depend on the use of Web standards and best practices. The basic concept behind designing with these is simple. Use the right tool for the job and adhere to its specifications. In Web standards, it is important that you separate content from presentation and behavior. Let me explain.

The three primary layers of websites are:

- Content and structure;

- Presentation; and

- Behavior.

The technologies used for creating the various layers of a mobile Web application are as follows:

Website "Layer"	Appropriate Technology
Content and Structure	HTML, HTML5, XHTML
Presentation	CSS
Behavior	JavaScript

The use of Web standards has long been a key to successful, professional Web design. As a learning developer, you have probably been shielded from these layers due to the rapid authoring tools or the development environment you use, so you may not be overly familiar with this triumvirate. Teaching this is beyond the scope of this book, but to truly deliver great mobile Web content, you will need to be familiar with the basics of Web design. I have a few favorite sources for gaining this familiarity. You should check these titles out to get more familiar with modern Web design tools and techniques.

Jennifer Niederst Robbins' book, *Learning Web Design,* serves as a great how-to manual for learning the ins and outs on Web design and offers lots of great examples. Jeffery Zeldman's *Designing with Web Standards* is a veritable Web design history lesson, and his narrative tells a great story about why Web standards matter. Other notable titles like Eric Meyer's *CSS: The Definitive Guide, 3rd Edition* and Mark Pilgrim's *HTML5: Up & Running* are worth the read and should not be ignored.

In addition to paying attention to Web standards, you are going to have to say goodbye to Web plugins. With uncertain support for common desktop plugins like Adobe Flash, Unity, Windows Media and QuickTime on mobile, you simply cannot depend on them for your content delivery. As we continue to obtain higher-performance devices with more capable just-in-time compilation and runtime interpretation of code (such as Mobile Safari's Nitro engine), it's not surprising that we will rely less and less on Web plugins. Why make reading harder when the devices are fully capable of handling the content with no additional downloads or installs? They're made to handle JavaScript in ways that desktop computers 10 years ago couldn't match. Because of its simple syntax and the fact that it is not a compiled language, but rather an interpreted one, it is easy to criticize JavaScript if you are coming from a strongly typed, object-oriented programming language. However, its overall ease of development and expressiveness in form is actually quite fun to work with. You need to try something new.

While mobile has led the way here, it's an inevitability that similar desktop procedures will follow. This should come as no surprise, and you should be used to evolutionary steps like this already. If you have been developing learning materials for any length of time, or if you work with people who have, then you have no doubt heard stories of changes in packaging content using standards such as SCORM and AICC. You are also probably familiar with the changes in development tools and programming languages for the Web like Authorware, Director, Flash and HTML5. If there is anything that is predictable about media handling on these devices, then it is that as time goes on, change will occur. You may have chosen the wrong field if you do not like change or learning new technologies. Change is a natural part of any profession dealing with technology today.

Likewise, if you are moving from a desktop delivery mechanism, and you are not looking to take full advantage of the new playground you have with mobile, then you need to lean on the brakes for a second. Pick up a mobile device, download the 25 top-rated apps in education, references, lifestyle and business and try them out. Do the same with the top mobile websites in your vertical market. There must be new ideas in each of them that you can apply to your content. Maybe it's a new navigation construct or an innovative use of the device's camera or accelerometer. These new features can seem esoteric for those who are new to the scene. Try this on the next mobile project you undertake: When you are considering the work to be done and how your information will be best distilled and disseminated, consider for just a moment whether this information would be easier to consume using a feature the device already provides. Perhaps it is your phone's built-in GPS or the ability to upload an image or video. Your exact circumstances will vary. The point is that until you think about how these new devices will make work easier for learners, using a tangible format, you will continue to develop learning materials in the same way you probably always have. This read-only, prepackaged, top-down form of getting information to your learners is changing. You must adapt. Try one or two small not-mission-critical functions and see what happens. You'll be surprised!

These devices are complex. They come with lots of features, storage, processing power and sensors. You should prepare yourself by reading up on this topic. Like understanding the basics of HTML, CSS and JavaScript, "grokking" (deeply understanding) gesture input is an art. This is another language and a distinctly different method of interacting with computing devices. I highly recommend you take time to read the excellent book by Dan Saffer, *Designing Gestural Interfaces: Touchscreens and Interactive Devices*. It does a great job of laying out the visual vocabulary and considerations you need to take into account when people start using your software in a direct, physical way. That's a hurdle for everyone as we move away from the mouse-and-keyboard world of the computer. Tasks are more immediate now. For example, the notion of removing the abstraction of the cursor and directly manipulating and interacting with on-screen elements is a new concept for most people. Throw away your conceptions about how drag-and-drop operations should feel. This is a new ball game. After you get several of the basics on how the input works, you will need to understand more on just how to design a pleasing experience as well. I recommend Steven Hoober's *Designing Mobile Interfaces* and Josh Clark's brilliant book, *Tapworthy*. Either one of these would be great by themselves, but when you master the information contained in both, you will be equipped to create amazing user interfaces for mobile websites and apps.

At this point, I might be singing a tune that you already know, but I repeat: know your audience. This includes their device hardware capabilities and OS versions. What are they capable of creating and consuming? You need to take this into account and target the devices and use their features, but plan to keep an eye to the future. Changes will happen. They will probably be improvements, but if your organization's policies shift and the BYOD (bring-your-own-device) policy they institute is less stringent or allows less-capable devices into the fold, you will need to be aware of this.

The shift away from "backwards compatibility" to "progressive enhancement" in the Web design and development community is just now starting to reverberate through the larger electronic communications industry, learning included. While you may be familiar with the concept of backwards compatibility, progressive enhancement probably seems obtuse or difficult to grasp. Both are similar on the surface but worlds apart at their core. Backwards compatibility is a well-intentioned, compassionate, yet somewhat misguided policy that forgives the shortcomings of a platform and requires the performers to dumb down their content and conventions in order to appeal to those on the lesser, all at the expense of the execution of a properly formed response to the use case at hand. On the other hand, progressive enhancement is an uncompromising yet permissive approach that gives the best to those who can access it but still provides a valuable experience for users of lower class devices and platforms in the target market. This difference is subtle, but marked. You have either the less-capable devices shaping the experience for all users, or have them informing them of their speed limit but allow them to use the niceties of the newer devices to create something advanced and wonderful for them, as long as the older devices get a usable experience.

We must remember that the core of our mission is not to simply dump a desktop experience onto a mobile site. Instead cut content, change input mechanisms, and switch interface metaphors. Do what you need to do to create the optimal solution for the people who are using your system and interacting with the content when they have the devices in hand. The navigation needs to be redesigned for mobile, at least, and all that might do is simply make your project usable. If you want to create a world-class project, you will need to expend a little effort to make the mobile interface and user experience into something special.

While it may not be a top-of-the-mind item for many in your company right now, there will come a time where the front line for information dissemination will be a mobile device. When your company introduces its next product, what is the first device your users will have in hand already? It may just be a smartphone or tablet. With this in mind, it's time to start entering the "mobile first" mindset. Most companies find it obvious that the mobile version of a site or product is no longer a phase 2 effort, but rather something that has to be considered right away. Because of this, the mobile design and development work should be happening concurrently with the development of the non-mobile end of the same project. If you neglect to put mobile first, it will be an afterthought and not get the appropriate attention needed to make it a success.

I started designing websites in 1996. Back then, almost nobody outside corporations and universities had broadband connections. The computer processing power was measured in megahertz. If you had more than 64 megabytes of RAM, you were on a powerful computer. In order to produce a usable, stable website, you had to make sure your site was optimized for delivery. This meant cleaning your HTML for extraneous garbage, choosing the appropriate asset types for your media, compressing these assets judiciously and tuning the server for optimal delivery.

Fast-forward to the current time, and the smartphones you have in your pocket are in many ways facing those same constraints. The hardware is less powerful than that of your desktop computer; the mobile data rate is usually far less than that of your cable modem or work broadband, and the total memory on your handheld is a fraction of what you have when you are at your desk. We must dust off our optimization skills and once again give careful consideration to the ways in which our media is crafted.

You can't simply dump a ton of content on your touchscreen like it's a big truck. You'll need to study the specifics of each platform you are delivering for to determine the appropriate formats, sizes and even scripting language specifics that each supports. For instance, a few devices might have image formats that use hardware acceleration for decoding them quickly, while other platforms might have kilobyte maximums for each page, and still others may have certain aspects of JavaScript that might or might not be supported. Checking your target platform's Web development guidelines before beginning your project's design phase is paramount.

The mobile Web is a tremendously exciting area in which to work and offers significant advantages over app delivery, but you do need to prepare for it in ways that you may not have considered when previously deploying eLearning modules.

DISTRIBUTING YOUR BUILDS (BETA OR RELEASE)

You need to have a way to distribute your mobile content to your users, be they testers or the final deployment audience. The methods for doing this vary depending on the tools you've used to create your product, the delivery format of app or Web and the user's device platform.

Let's explore a few options. Take a look at the following matrix:

Platform	App	Web
iOS	Requires UDID	Open; Can be restricted via username/password, IP address and more
Android	Open (requires some device configuration)	Open; Can be restricted via username/password, IP address and more
BlackBerry	Requires debug token	Open; Can be restricted via username/password, IP address and more
Windows Phone	Requires signed app for store, but not for beta	Open; Can be restricted via username/password, IP address and more

App and Web deployment options

As you can see, it's not too complex, but it will require a little planning. Make sure you have the pieces in place during the initial Alpha and Beta testing to ensure a smooth transition. Don't let the distribution phase be what makes or breaks your project.

Consider these as you prepare for delivery:

- Security, security, security;

- Give expectations to your users;

- Provide release notes;

- Provide expiring builds and revoke access; and

- Know who is going to see your content.

It should go without saying, but you have to protect your organization's intellectual property and investment. Your build distribution mechanism needs to be accessible and usable but also secure. Work with your technology team to make sure that you are following proper protocol. This may require using your intranet, SharePoint site or other tools. If you don't currently have a platform or policy in place, work with one or two partners to develop one. You'll want to follow best practice.

Let your users know what they are getting and how to get it. Many users have not had experiences with Beta software or installed apps through any other method aside from the typical app store installation method. You'll need to provide detailed explanations on how the install procedures will work and what, if any, content may be missing or incomplete. The same goes for features and any or all bugs. This is a document typically referred to in the software industry as the release notes. It's used to relay any information specific to the software build. This could include the installation instructions, new features, and known issues. It should also include a basic changelog or version history so that your users have some context for what has been improved since the last update. Related to this, remember to put a build number or test run number somewhere in a visible part of the application so that that testers know what version they are using. Typically, you can put this on the application's splash screen or inside an *About This App* screen or settings panel. You can be discrete; just be distinct.

Any builds during the development and testing phase need to be able to expire and/or be revoked. Of course, you don't want old or out-of-date builds running during testing phases, as you will not get accurate test data or have the ability to distinguish the issues that are being logged from current or legacy builds. You also don't want out-of-date content or intellectual property escaping the friendly confines of your organization. You need a plan in place to make sure that content can expire when needed, old builds can be killed when new ones come out, and testers who leave the testing program can have their access revoked. You're right to think that these are not trivial plans to make, but they are the types of problems that a developer loves to solve. Once an issue has been solved for a particular deployment model, it's been fixed for other projects that follow. Bottom line: It's a problem worth fixing.

The fact is that you don't want anonymous testers and reviewers for your initial builds. You need to be able to verify the identities of your testers in order to protect your content, get the feedback that you need and also potentially remove those who fail to give it their all. Password protection is a first step, and perhaps a bit too restrictive. You can make a few additions that won't come off as annoying to your testers as having them log in every time they launch the app. Perhaps you can restrict testers' access to specific time periods or require the app to be used at specific geolocation coordinates. Beyond that, you can also tie builds to device IDs such as UDIDs on Apple devices or even IMEI on other makers' devices. If you haven't gotten feedback logs from specific testers, consider prompting them when they launch the website or log into the app or service. If continued absentee testing occurs, you can take further action after a proper process of warning and recommendations. It sounds a bit like monitoring a child, but when testers are repeatedly told they need to identify themselves in order to participate, maybe – just maybe – they will.

APPLICATION DEPLOYMENT TOOLS

At this point in your mobile strategy, you have chosen a platform for your organization, procured the devices, developed your mobile policies, and provisioned the devices for deployment. The devices are in your users' hands, and you need to get your apps and media to them. Publishing your information is the next step in your mobile planning.

Let's talk first about how to do this with mobile apps.

Publishing your mobile apps and media inside your organization can require significant planning. There are a number of steps to consider from the deployment process to updating and securing the apps. In your mobile strategy, you need to find a distribution method that allows for you to manage these steps.

Getting apps and media on mobile devices has typically been done using one of three methods. There is the online marketplace method, such as Apple's App Store or Google Play, which is effective for getting apps to a large and widespread user base, but it is only suitable for consumer media and applications. There are also many app marketplaces from both the mobile platform developers and third-party sources. Your organization would either need to choose which marketplace best serves your needs, or use several and monitor and maintain your apps on each system.

Enterprise apps – with sensitive or confidential information or a limited number of targeted users – probably don't fit in a publicly available distribution method. Another method for publishing your organization's apps and media is ad hoc installation. On various platforms, this is also known as sideloading or manual installation. Ad hoc installation requires downloading the application installer or media file and manually installing it on each mobile device. Some platforms are easier to manage manually than others, but users could find the process confusing or too time-consuming to keep their apps up to date.

The other method is to build a private app catalog to install apps wirelessly. This is sometimes called OTA, or over-the-air installation. A private app catalog lets you distribute your apps and media to mobile devices in a more user-friendly manner. The original problem with this method was that it was just an automated way to perform ad hoc distribution. Users would receive an email or SMS text that contained a link to their organization's private app server. They had to hit that link, download the installer, and put the application on their devices manually. It helped to get apps to users and a geographically diverse user base faster without putting them in a public marketplace, but there was still no way to tell if people downloaded and installed the apps or files. In the enterprise IT world, organizations need to know what is installed where and ensure that proper updates occur for security and licensing requirements. How can you make that happen in mobile?

The prevalent answer to that question is to use mobile application management (MAM) software. Mobile application management systems allow organizations to create a private application catalog that works similar to the public marketplaces. Media files and documents that are useful to mobile users can often be included in an MAM system as well. Apps can be categorized and only visible to specific users, as they would in traditional enterprise application-deployment systems. If the MAM platform supports it, then apps can be updated either by notifying mobile users or even by push updates without user intervention. If a user leaves the organization, or has accessed the application improperly, apps can be removed or disabled from mobile devices without requiring a full device wipe. This can give you more flexibility in making sure mobile devices comply with your policies.

Mobile application development can also benefit from having an application management system in place. When it comes time to test on actual devices, being able to publish updates for each build is easier than connecting each device and loading an app manually. This can dramatically speed up the development process in your organization.

MAM systems can also be helpful in monitoring and ensuring compliance with application licensing. Your mobile systems administrator can use an MAM's reporting features to see which users have installed apps or downloaded available media, and keep track of or limit how many users install a specific app to comply with licensing requirements. In conjunction with a mobile device management (MDM) system, you can have a variety of tools to keep your organization in compliance with your mobile strategy. MDM is not the same as MAM, however. Several mobile device management platforms offer application management features, but a dedicated mobile application management system usually has more features and will serve your organization better.

Mobile application management is a tool that can help with your organization's mobile applications lifecycle from development and testing to deployment and updating. With a bit of planning, MAM can make it easier to publish the apps and media in your organization.

If you typically shy away from commercial solutions and like to take a more DIY approach, you certainly can. Make sure you use HTTPS and password protection, and send the link to your app to your testers or even your final users. It lacks the bells and whistles, and it could be a long-term maintenance issue due to versioning or anything else that could pop up. Its ease of deployment and overall flexibility still make it a viable option.

If you are not targeting internal application distribution, but rather the actual app stores or marketplaces, you will be best served by reading up on the process for each. Attempting to cover all of them in this book would be a fool's errand. Not only are there many ways to do this with each tool, but the rules change with every release. This section of the book would be out of date even before it went to print.

MEASURING THE IMPACT OF YOUR CONTENT

Now that your mobile learning project is out, we can get to the important stuff: measurement. This is the cornerstone of basic eLearning content evaluation. What did you think of the content in this lesson/course? Was it effectively relayed? Did you learn something you can apply upon returning to work? We've all seen this model before. This is the foundation for the most common method of evaluation in learning and development used today: the Kirkpatrick model.

Taking it up a notch, you might be led to a line of questions like these: Do you use the newly acquired skills from working with the app on the job? How have you applied your learning? Has your learning experience proven valuable in improving your performance? There will also possibly be outside evaluation by the person's supervisor or manager along the same lines. This is the second level of the Kirkpatrick model.

Beyond that, we need to measure behavior and business results. These are Kirkpatrick's levels three and four respectively. Did this information cause you to change your habits or perform in a new way? Did the usage of this information lead to increased productivity, accuracy, or safety? One of the upshots of mobile learning is that because it is applied at the point of need, you are by almost all accounts jumping right to level three and level four evaluations. This is because you can draw direct relationships between a learner's access to the information and its use to affect behavior and achieve business results. While some may argue whether or not this is indeed learning evaluation or something else entirely, I will leave that out of this discussion. However, one cannot argue with the results. Mobile learning *does* lead to increased performance.

In creating a framework for measurement, we need to step outside the box. Begin to consider an alternative means of measuring your content development's effectiveness.

Learning management systems (LMSs) provides many metrics that learning professionals employ every day to see how learning materials are being used and the effect they have on their organizations. However, with the advent of mLearning, several changes that have upset the proverbial apple cart are taking place. For better or worse, many mobile learning applications simply don't run with current LMS implementations. Furthermore, many traditional eLearning measures, such as mastery, completion and course duration, don't apply to mobile learning because of its just-in-time nature. These are all vestiges of the concepts of "just-in-case" or "ahead-of-time" learning, not just-in-time information delivery.

This key difference in the reason for putting learning content online in a mobile-accessible format should be a tipoff that the previous methods for measurement may need re-evaluation. People often use mobile learning applications for quick reference, performance support, and job aids. These use cases are usually much more application-like than immersive media frameworks, AJAX, and mobile applications via any number of software analytics platforms is easy. When applied to mobile learning, these events could log the users' geolocational data, the OS and/or platform they are on, their corporate ID, or whether they searched or browsed to get to the target data they needed. To determine whether your content is well designed and providing assistance at the point of need, you can record user session length, bounce rate, and the top content accessed.

Another aspect to examine would be the post-support or sales event logging. If your sales personnel or technician needs to update a CRM or other ticketing application after a meeting or house call, perhaps there is an opportunity to add fields to the ticketing screen that ask if they used mobile help. A follow-up field could ask what content they accessed or if it was helpful. Make these fields a required entry prior to logging the event and you instantly have data points to determine whether your mobile learning materials are helping for the target audience. Use this information to inform your revisions and additions, and continue to check in to see if the overall evaluation of your software improves.

One way to measure the success of your performance support is to consider that you would like your organization's employees to rely on it less and less. This is not an issue if the software is support for changing information. Cross-tabulating usage records with employee IDs and feedback you have received can show if your cleverly crafted mLearning is resulting in more retention and hopefully more confident and capable employees. Perhaps another area to look at is support-center calls. Are they decreasing after putting your knowledge base online in mobile format? Are the types of calls that would be considered Level 1 or easy dropping off? These types of performance-support measurements don't require an LMS at all, but they show the effectiveness of your deployment.

As a learning professional who uses metrics to inform your design decisions, you may believe that moving learning content outside your LMS ties your hands. In reality, when you decouple the content from the existing forms of measurement and reconsider what it truly is that you want to measure, you may find that mobile learning is actually an empowering way for you to see the effectiveness of your instructional design. You'll also learn how it affects your learners' day-to-day operations, and in turn have measurable results, regardless of whether or not they are stored in an LMS.

GETTING FEEDBACK

A key factor in any agile effort is to get feedback so that you may measure its success and build upon it. This can be done in a wide variety of ways. A few of these you may be doing already in your courses and learning development. These are the traditional smilies, if you will. This form of basic evaluation – "Did you like this course? Did this course present new information? Can you use information in this course to help you with your daily tasks?" – are all still valid, though they may require some rewriting to fit the new model of your delivery.

This shouldn't be thought of as the endpoint for getting feedback or measuring the effects of your learning content, and it certainly isn't the end for mobile. You can get so much additional feedback through other means. If your app is deployed to public marketplaces, you can easily ask your learners to use the built-in rating systems. Prompting them to do so is not difficult; in fact, it's a common way for developers to seed their ratings in the game market. If you have an app distribution platform like an MAM or MDM system in place, a few of them also have this type of functionality built in. It's also not beyond reason to consider building this feature into your app.

Beyond traditional mobile rating tools like these, there are a multitude of other options you can use. Online surveying tools such as SurveyMonkey and Zoomerang have made it simple to create, share and embed surveys into a myriad of formats. You can tuck the feedback into a settings screen or info panel, and you're at least a little closer to getting information back on what your users thought about the content and the delivery. Voila! Instant smilies!

Here are some quick points to consider about this path:

- Get feedback that ties directly to your learning objectives and goals for the project. "Did you like the content in this app?" is not good. "Did the content in this app help you get your job done quicker or easier?" is better.

- Don't ask too many questions. Two to five questions is enough to get information you can use. Any more and you are pushing it.

- Feel free to nag your learner with a dialog asking for feedback after a few launches, but allow them a way to opt out of the nags for good as well.

- Build a feedback link into the app's about or info screen. You should try to obtain a volume of information in order to have a few touchstones from a qualitative standpoint. Make the feedback process as easy as possible. If you can afford it, and if your privacy policy allows, try to use a commercial service such as UserVoice to capture and quantify the demand for changes and features.

- If it's not against your privacy policies or other terms of use, try to find ways to correlate the input you get from your users with the usage analytics you are also gathering via built-in tracking.

After you have some basic surveying in place you'll start to get input right away. Let's make sure that you have plans in place to act on the feedback. Build, measure, and adjust – right?

REVISING CONTENT

I hope you have thick skin. Getting feedback can be tough to take. I have great news, though: With mobile, it's usually easy to make adjustments and deploy new builds.

This shift is the norm for Web content developers. Not as much for learning developers who commonly think that a piece of launched content is perfect. As far as they're concerned, it's fully formed and ready for consumption. It's been carefully crafted with participation of an SME. It's been run through legal and compliance. It *has* to be perfect. It doesn't need to be changed or modified.

Of course this is not true. An entire industry based around content management systems, or CMS, has arisen since the early days of the Web. The Web is a fluid medium, changing as the climate around it changes. How many times have you adjusted the usual eLearning course in your library after deployment? Yeah, I thought so. They usually launch, get used and lie dormant until they get completely reworked and relaunched.

This simply doesn't work when applied to the mindset behind mobile. The mobile market changes quickly. Devices change, platforms change, and the information on the devices change as people expect them to do. You need to revise the content, edit the website or app, and publish it again as quickly as possible.

If you have in place an MDM or MAM solution – which are made for these situations – this is already familiar territory. The same applies to Web content management. We are used to pushing out new content and assets regularly, sometimes daily or even more often. With your own application-distribution platform you will not be subject to app store approval cycles or timelines.

You can change your content, and you should. Don't be concerned about users finding it or getting lost in your application as features change from launch to launch. If you designed your application within the parameters of what your users were looking for and what the delivery platform dictates as best practices, then you have nothing to be concerned about. One of the primary reasons we never revised or moved new content into a lot of existing eLearning content was not because of the regulatory or other external stakeholder groups; it was due to the fact that we never adhered to a strong standard of user interface or user experience design. Because of this, whenever you added a new piece of content or moved something from one section to another, it would require sending everything through the entire approval chain. This recurring pain caused us to stop pushing through incremental changes, and we simply waited for the big change to get approved.

Mobile's connected or cloud nature and the transient nature of typical just-in-time content provides us the capability to be more flexible in making changes to our existing content. A good percentage of applications have content that comes from the Web in a service or other downloadable format. There is no reason any longer to wait for release due to optical media replication or shipping, so any legacy release schedule is now null and void. Desktop OSs and plugins are also no longer a factor, and therefore, their release schedules and associate security updates are also not a concern. The typical mobile OS patch or update takes far less time than the usual corporate PC timeline for the same sort of feature additions. Users are becoming more accustomed to shorter release cycles. Let the content delivery and revision cycles accelerate with them.

Your learners will appreciate the currency of the content. Your developers will enjoy the velocity. Your legal and compliance teams might thank you as well.

ADDING FEATURES

Awesome! You have made it to phase two, version 1.5 or whatever you are calling the next release of your product. You must have done something right. Your users found your content valuable, and your stakeholders have given you a new lease on life and a new milestone to reach.

This is a great time to celebrate and reflect on everything you accomplished and learned in the first version of your application. Pull out the notes you made. Dust off the binder containing all of the suggestions you received after you locked the scope for the first version. You are going to need these.

In addition to the features you and your team dreamed up, you probably have a number of user-requested features. Hopefully you have been trapping these as well. If you didn't have a support forum or feedback link in your product, you didn't follow my advice.

Now that you have your desired features listed, it's time to produce a road map and have a next phase development card-sorting exercise or feature discussion. Much has been written on the agile process as already mentioned, so I won't try to go into detail here, but the basic premise for reviewing your desired features and the ones submitted by your users would be to determine their overall value and compare that to the projected effort needed to develop them further. Typically each feature is assigned a value for both its perceived business worth and the estimated effort to create it. The values are tabulated, and items that are easy to implement, but have high business value, are usually added to a list of tasks that will be built in the next development revision, or sprint. The process of evaluating and weighting possible features goes on until a development sprint of sufficient length – often measured in weeks and usually less than two to three months – is created. Only then can design and development commence.

Once the sprint is underway, no new features or items can be added. The scope is locked until the next release and the subsequent measure-and-revise sequence begins. This sort of methodology is different for learning professionals, but it is used in nearly all major mobile development firms. It offers a great deal of agility and maintains required velocity. The work is user-driven at its core; after all, they're the ones that are speaking up. The development team then assesses and responds to them by giving the market what they want. Imagine how effective your learning materials could be if they were shaped by the demands of the learners combined with the guidance of your SMEs and instructional designers. I'm getting choked up just thinking about it.

IN SUMMARY

The deployment and distribution of your mobile learning is going to feel different. After all, it is developed for a different form factor and with different goals. The user experience is different, and the user interface is different. You have a whole new world opened to you with the mobile Web. It offers challenges for those that have gotten used to the desktop and don't often venture into the world of their source code, so you may have a bit of a learning curve – or maybe an unlearning curve.

Getting your builds to your testers should not be difficult. You need to make sure that you set your expectations and your users understand them when you are putting testing software into their hands. Release notes, known issues, security and lots of other problems need to be taken care of before you start launching products.

Once you have these in place, you will need some assistance in placing your application in the hands of your users. You can do this with products or services like MAM or MDM, but if your needs are relatively simple, you can also do this with a dash of gumption and a spritz of trial and error. There are detailed guides on how to implement an enterprise distribution of your products as well as guides for getting your apps into the marketplaces themselves.

With the products in the field, you need to gather and measure feedback, stowing it away for your next release. Your next release should be a blend of weighted features meant to maximize business results and improvements to the user experience that sustain interest and focus on the product. You can add features, but continue to maintain the velocity and rigor in terms of scope and schedule that you did on the first builds.

FOURTEEN

PUTTING IT
ALL TOGETHER

REALIZING THE BENEFITS

We've arrived. You now have a thorough understanding of the benefits of mobile learning. You now understand the differences between augmentation and presentation of materials and how this distinction applies to this field. If you plan on leveraging mobile technology for learning, then you need to understand these two concepts and relay their finer points to your management.

Once you have the green light, review your goals and determine what the audience needs. Your mobile learning materials may be snippets of information, delivered as performance support or perhaps entirely new materials delivered to users in the field. You may need to move some of your existing learning content to a mobile format, because this will maximize productivity and regain some of the time lost when employees travel or are otherwise inaccessible. In many ways mobile learning is about doing more with less, but if you fail to take the time to understand your audience's needs, you could miss the mark by delivering something that hasn't been requested. Maximize workers' productivity by maximizing your effort. You may have some content in your learning library that could benefit from being freed from the desktop. Just because it's a new medium doesn't mean you always need to reinvent the wheel.

When first approaching a subject as big as mobile learning, you will need to spend some time creating a content strategy. This strategy should take a holistic view of your current library, your application portfolio, your overall business goals, and your learners and their needs. To stave off the flood of apps and the inevitable lackluster results that will emerge if you approach mobile learning without sufficient forethought, you must also have a content strategy in place as part of your overall plan. This is just as much about the creation and curation of the content as it is about its ongoing governance and maintenance.

As part of solidifying a content strategy, your assessment should take into account the value of the content you have, its applicability to your mobile learners, and the effort needed to make it mobile-ready. Through this careful process, certain trends will emerge, and you should be able to choose some quick wins for your organization. Consider while planning how the ROI will be measured and what you need to do in order to meet the expectations of your business partners.

The content you choose to develop into mobile learning materials should be structured based on your delivery format. In my experience, mobile learning typically fits into one of the four categories I presented earlier. You have content forming up to create a wide variety of possible mLearning delivery methods – all comprised of business process software, peer-based or social learning, conversions from other sources, and learning content made possible via the devices' unique affordances.

Each of these content types has distinct use cases and corresponding user interface design patterns that offer the best overall user experience. You need to recognize when the content you are working with falls into one of these categories and design the interface to match it. Creating an interface without the content or content strategy in place is a recipe for disaster. Your design will be unfocused and the users' tasks will be secondary to the on-screen UI. You want the interface to fade into the background around the content itself, not the other way around.

With content strategy and interface design in place, build something to take to your learners as a prototype, then a pilot. You'll need to set up a team and a process. This team and the development process may differ from those of your previous experiences in building learning, so you must be prepared to make that shift. Move on to a larger rollout after your pilots have proven successful.

In mobile you are going to need to explore more agile methods that allow you to go to market quicker and with greater rigor in terms of scope definition and adherence. Missing deadlines in mobile can often derail efforts entirely. Stay on focus and keep your delivery dates. You can always add features and content later.

You will be wading into a new world of technology, and there is much to learn. The differences between mobile Web and mobile apps need to be understood. The intricacies of user interface and user experiences across platforms – and with it, the process needed to create those planning documents such as sketches, wireframes and mockups – is a skill that will need to be honed in your team. One interface does not fit all, so trying to cram a tablet UI into a phone or vice versa is not something you will want to do. There are many tools out there to create Web and mobile apps. This analysis phase is valuable and can save you time and effort later, so be sure to understand what it is you need to create, and make certain the tool fully supports your vision.

With anything new it's often wise to try out prototypes and pilots. Mobile is no different. You have to enter these first endeavors with clear goals and end targets in mind. A pilot or prototype lacking direction and a mission is set up to fail. Choose your platforms and testers from representatives of your target group, not from the early adopters or the geeks alone. They are the ones most likely to give you the best results for your tests. You need a representative sampling of the various personalities from your overall end user base in order to get an accurate reading.

Product deployment can be stressful. Be sure to do some planning on your deployment before you create the first pixel or even deliver the first designs to your stakeholders. This should not hold you up at the last minute. Plan to have software processes and measurement tools in place from the start. Obtain both quantitative and qualitative feedback from your users in order to understand the overall perception of your work, and recognize available areas for improvement.

After your version 1.0 has landed and is in use, it's time to dust off those features and requests you have fielded.

BUILDING ON YOUR SUCCESS

The best part about launching a successful product is that you are going to become a popular project lead for all the upcoming mobile learning projects sure to come. This could be seen in a bad light. After all, you are going to be busy, right?

You have just delivered something great, but the journey isn't over yet. You might have launched a pilot. If so, consider moving to a larger pilot. If it has been successful, it's time to push your app out to a larger audience. Go with a workgroup or business-unit deployment or perhaps push for an enterprise-wide deployment.

Once you have out an app or two that exhibits some basic features, it's time to get adventurous. You can start to roll out advanced features such as augmented reality and geolocation, use the device storage, and start to push the limits. You will be surprised at just how quickly your learners get it. Mobile technology advances have largely been driven by the consumer market, after all, and people seem to be getting comfy with their devices, as seen by the user base of the augmented reality apps such as Layar and the popularity of Foursquare. You don't need to shy away from the device features as you may have in the past with PC learning content.

This is all heartening, especially so when you realize just how early we are in the whole lifespan of the mobile revolution. The International Data Corporation (2011) estimated that 1 billion smartphones will ship in 2015. Beyond that, the Pew Research Center revealed in April of 2012 that only 21 percent of adults in the United States have read an e-book (Rainie, Zickuhr, Purcell, Madden, & Brenner, 2012). The market is growing quickly and has quite a way to go before we have truly reached saturation. With this much market left to expand into, it is easy to see that learning how to design and develop your own mobile learning applications and Web apps is going to be a worthwhile skill to attain.

IN SUMMARY

That's all there is to it. You have just begun, so continue along the path and create your best learning content. Your learners will thank you, and your organization will, too. This content might be traditional learning on the mobile device, but there is more room to explore. Everything from business process and productivity to informal and social learning are the domain of mobile. This is a big world, and it's always accessible with your learners having a powerful tool like mobile devices in their pockets or on their hips. It truly is about learning everywhere.

APPENDIX A

GLOSSARY

To find terms more specific to mobile learning, please download the free Float Mobile Learning Primer available for iOS and Android at http://floatlearning.com/apps/.

Accelerometer: An accelerometer measures the acceleration of the device. Among other things, the accelerometer is used to present landscape or portrait views of a screen based on the way the device is being held.

ADDIE model: A traditional process used by instructional designers and training developers composed of five phases – Analysis, Design, Development, Implementation and Evaluation.

Affordance: A quality or feature of something to allow users to perform an action.

Ad hoc distribution: Ad hoc distribution allows you to test an application before it's available in an app store. You can use this to share applications with beta users.

Agile development: A software development method in which software is iterative and incremental because of its adaptive and flexible nature. Agile development succeeds at preventing scope creep because of the planning that goes into the development phase.

Ambient light sensors: "Ambient light sensors are used to detect light or brightness in a manner similar to the human eye. They are most commonly found in industrial lighting, consumer electronics, and automotive systems, where they allow settings to be adjusted automatically in response to changing ambient light conditions. By turning on, turning off, or adjusting features, ambient light sensors can conserve battery power or provide extra safety while eliminating the need for manual adjustments" (Ambient Light Sensors, p. 2).

Application programming interface (API): A particular set of rules and specifications that a software program can follow to access and make use of the services and resources provided by another software program that implements that API. APIs from Facebook and Twitter, for example, allow developers to create a plethora of applications.

Asynchronous JavaScript and XML (AJAX): A group of interrelated Web development methods used on the client side to create interactive Web applications. With AJAX, Web applications can retrieve data from the server asynchronously in the background without interfering with the display and behavior of the existing page. It's used frequently in mobile Web development.

Augmented reality (AR): A term for a live or an indirect view of a physical, real-world environment whose elements are augmented by computer-generated sensory input, such as text, sound or graphics. Layar, Urbanspoon and many other mobile apps are successfully using AR in conjunction with location services to provide mobile learning.

Aviation Industry Computer-Based Training Committee (AICC): An international association of technology-based training professionals.

Backwards compatibility: The ability for a newer device to receive input generated by an older device. An example would be that games originally available for the PlayStation console can also be played on a PlayStation 2.

Bespoke applications: Apps developed for a custom purpose and built to a customer's specification. They are not released to any app store. The term originates from tailoring, where bespoke clothing and shoes are made exactly to the buyer's desired fit and using their chosen fabrics.

Big data: A term used for data sets so large that commonly used software cannot effectively handle them.

Binary file: A file that may contain any type of data, encoded in binary form (0s and 1s) for computer storage and processing purposes.

BlackBerry Messenger (BBM): BlackBerry's proprietary instant messaging app allowing BlackBerry users to communicate with each other.

Bluetooth: Bluetooth allows users to exchange data over short distances with low amounts of power. Bluetooth is different from Wi-Fi and can be used to connect wireless headsets to your mobile device, as well as sync with other devices.

Bounce rate: In Web traffic analysis, the percentage of visitors who enter the site and leave before visiting other pages on the site.

Bring your own device (BYOD): A policy where businesses let employees use their own personal phones or tablets. Companies save the expense of purchasing the devices, but procurement gets significantly more difficult with the array of devices used by employees.

Build: The result of compiling source code into software.

Bytecode: A highly optimized format of translated code tuned to ensure proper playback for a specific platform. This happens when native apps are compiled.

Canny edge detection: An algorithm developed by John Canny that can process and detect edges in images.

Cascading Stylesheets (CSS): A stylesheet language that determines how display a document written in a markup language. CSS is most commonly used to style Web pages written in HTML and XHTML.

CSS3: The latest specification of CSS. CSS3 allows Web designers to create mobile-friendly themes and includes advanced stylistic and animation features. CSS3 is a component of the HTML5 technology set.

Changelog: A record of changes made to a website or to software. This record could include new features, bug fixes or known issues.

Check-ins: A phrase commonly referred to in social networks, where "checking-in" equates to announcing or logging your presence at a physical location or event.

Cloud: Cloud computing refers to providing computational resources on demand via a network.

Cloud instance: A phrase typically used to describe a virtual machine or specific cloud server created for a single purpose. The term "instance" usually refers to an Amazon EC2 server.

Console: A term used to describe a developer tool that allows users to search through all of the system's messages, and can alert the user when certain types of messages occur.

Customer relationship management (CRM): The act of organizing and synchronizing a company's interactions with potential clients, current clients and other contacts by using software.

Didactic: Something designed or intended to teach.

Doc: Short for document. May also refer to a Microsoft Word document, as .doc or .docx are file extension options.

Eclipse: An open-source, extensible development environment often used for Java technologies, and commonly used by Android developers.

Electronic Performance Support System (EPSS): "An EPSS is the electronic infrastructure that captures, stores and distributes individual and corporate knowledge assets throughout an organization to enable individuals to achieve required levels of performance in the fastest possible time and with a minimum of support from other people" (Raybould, 1995).

Emulator: An emulator imitates running one system on another system. In mobile design and development, use of an emulator may be required in order to test prerelease hardware or OS builds, or in order to test on a wide variety of systems to which you may not have direct access. For example, it's possible to run an iOS simulator on an Apple computer using the Mac OS.

Enterprise resource planning (ERP): ERP software is used to manage the processes of large organizations.

Extensible hypertext markup language (XHTML): An XML-based variant of the HTML family of Web markup languages.

Extensible Markup Language (XML): A simple text-based format for representing structured information: documents, data, configuration, books, transactions, invoices and much more.

Frequently Asked Questions (FAQ): A list of common questions and answers that many users have about a product or service.

Friendster: One of the original social networking platforms. Originally launched in 2002, it ascended to more 3 million users shortly after launch. Its popularity has waned since its peak in 2008, and has since been rebranded as a gaming site after its buyout by MOL Global in 2009.

File transfer protocol (FTP): Allows for files to be transferred from one host to another over a network such as the Internet. Typically, FTP is used to transfer Web pages from a private development machine to a public server.

Geocaching: A game based on hiding something (usually a physical object) in a location that is to be found by someone later. Geocaching participants usually use GPS to find the hidden objects.

Geofence: A virtual perimeter for a real-world geographic area.

Geolocation: The geographic identification of an object, such as a mobile device, in the real world, usually with the use of GPS technology.

Gestural input: Input interpreted by a device or operating system in response to one or more touch or movement events. For example, a user rotates two fingers simultaneously, and the device or operating system interprets that touch input as a rotation gesture. Some gestures are performed with one finger or touch point, while other gestures require multiple touch points. The device or operating system establishes the type of gesture to assign to the input. Both touch and gesture input can be multitouch input, depending on the user's device.

Global Positioning System (GPS): A space-based navigation system developed and maintained by the United States government. A person can pinpoint his or her location using a GPS receiver, which obtains information from several satellites.

Grok: To thoroughly know or understand something. Robert Heinlein, an American science fiction writer, coined the term in his 1961 novel, "Stranger in a Strange Land."

Gyroscope: "A gyroscope can be used to either measure, or maintain, the orientation of a device," says mobile author Alasdair Allan. "Unlike an accelerometer, which measures the linear acceleration of the device, a gyroscope measures the orientation directly. When the iPhone's accelerometer measurements are combined with the gyroscope measurements, developers can create applications that can sense motion on six-axes: up and down, left and right, forward and backwards, as well as the roll, pitch and yaw rotations" (Slocum, 2010).

H.264: A standard of high-definition video recording, compression and distribution.

Human performance improvement (HPI): William J. Rothwell, professor of workforce education and development at Penn State, defines HPI as "the systematic process of discovering and analyzing important human performance gaps, planning for future improvements in human performance, designing and developing cost-effective and ethically justifiable solutions to close performance gaps, implementing the solutions, and evaluating the financial and nonfinancial results" (as cited in *Human Performance Improvement)*.

Hypertext markup language (HTML): A basic building block of the World Wide Web. This document format and syntax provides structure to content and is the most commonly found method for displaying Web pages.

Hypertext transfer protocol secure (HTTPS): An encrypted, protected, secure version of hypertext transfer protocol (HTTP).

Information architecture (IA): "Information architecture is a discipline and a set of methods that aim to identify and organize information in a purposeful and service-oriented way," says Michael Cummings (2009), a user experience designer. "It is also a term used to describe the resulting document or documents that define the facets of a given information domain. The goal of information architecture is to improve information access, relevancy and usefulness to a given audience, as well as improve the publishing entity's ability to maintain and develop the information over time. It is primarily associated with website design and it is directly related to the following professional disciplines: User interface design, content development, content management, usability engineering, interaction design, and user experience design. It is also indirectly related to database design, document design and knowledge management."

Integrated development environment (IDE): A software application that provides comprehensive facilities to computer programmers for software development. An IDE normally consists of a source code editor, build automation tools and a debugger. A couple examples of IDEs are Xcode and Eclipse.

Instructor-led training (ILT): Training typically given in a classroom, lab or work site training area and facilitated by a trainer or other learning professional.

IM: Instant message.

iMessage: Apple's instant messenger service for iOS5 and OS X Mountain Lion.

Instructional systems design (ISD): Instructional design, also known as instructional systems design, is "a technology which incorporates known and verified learning strategies into instructional experiences which make the acquisition of knowledge and skill more efficient, effective, and appealing" (Merrill, Drake, Lacy, & Pratt, 1996, p. 6).

International mobile equipment identity (IMEI): Used to identify various phones.

Internet relay chat (IRC): A protocol for real-time Internet text messaging or conferencing.

.IPA: The file extension of an application archive file that stores an iOS app.

JavaScript Object Notation (JSON): An open, text-based data exchange format similar to XML that is language-independent, meaning it can be parsed by a number of applications. For example, one use of JSON is in AJAX-based Web applications. JSON uses conventions similar to those found in C, C++, C#, Java, JavaScript, Perl or Python.

Kirkpatrick's four levels of learning evaluation: Reaction, learning, behavior, results. Developed by Donald Kirkpatrick, a former president of the American Society for Training and Development, this model evaluates training courses' effectiveness.

Learning management system (LMS) / Learning content management system (LCMS): An LMS/LCMS is a multi-user environment where learning developers can create, store, reuse, manage and deliver digital learning content from a central object repository.

Learner record store (LRS): A place to store learning records. An LRS can interface with an LMS for reporting purposes.

Manual installation: A non-automatic way of putting software on a device.

Mobile application management (MAM): The remote administration of apps, media and configuration profiles without having to manage the devices themselves.

Mobile device management (MDM): A way for a company or group to manage mobile devices. This includes how they are configured and how they fit in with the policies of an IT department.

MediaWiki: Free, open-source wiki software used by Wikipedia, as well as other wikis.

Metacognition: Knowing about knowing. In other words, this is knowledge of one's own cognitive processes. J. H. Flavell popularized the concept in 1976. **Metadata:** Data about data. For example, who created the data? When was it created? How was it created? Where are the data?

Multitouch: Touching two or more points on a particular surface and having the device recognize those touches.

Near-field communication (NFC): A set of short-range wireless technologies that connects devices. NFC targets take very simple form factors such as tags, stickers, key fobs, or cards that do not require batteries. NFC peer-to-peer communication is also possible, where both devices are powered.

.Net Framework: A software framework developed by Microsoft that runs primarily on Microsoft Windows and Windows Phones.

NoSQL: A lightweight, open-source relational database that doesn't use the standard SQL interface.

Objection-handling wizard: A software program to assist with the overall process to handle objections.

Operating system (OS): Software consisting of programs and data that runs on computers, manages computer hardware resources and provides common services for efficient execution of various application software. OSs are found on almost any device with a computer, from video game consoles to smartphones to tablets.

Orkut: Launched in 2004, Orkut is one of the oldest social networking sites still in operation today. Google now owns Orkut.

Over-the-air (OTA) installation: The process of installing software without requiring a physical connection to the device.

Pageview: A request to load an HTML file of a website. In other words, a pageview would be counted when a user visited the page.

PDF: An open, universally readable file format created by Adobe Systems Inc.

Performant: Computer jargon for exhibiting the performance expected and operating normally.

Persona: Fictional people created for a user-centered design process. These characters contain demographic, attitude and behavior details in them that help the designer consider ways that their creation may be used.

PhpWiki: A Web-based wiki software system built using the programming language PHP.

Personal learning network (PLN): This informal network helps people make connections in order to learn from each other.

Plugin: A Web browser module used to extend the functionality of the Web browser to handle new media types, interaction models or other functionality not included with the browser's stock download state.

Progressive enhancement: A Web design and development method that stresses semantic HTML markup, accessibility and external stylesheets and scripting, meaning those tools would be called from another file. This lets everyone access basic functionality and content.

Quick response (QR) code: A special barcode that can be scanned by mobile devices in order to quickly link to URLs, contact information or other media.

Random access memory (RAM): A typically volatile form of computer data storage. This fast type of memory is used to store information currently in use, or recently in use in the device.

Really simple syndication (RSS): Web feeds published in an incremented, standardized format.

Regression: Occurs when a change causes a previously fixed bug or software issue to reappear and the software reverts to a previous error condition.

Release notes: Documents distributed with software notifying users of changes or bugs.

Request for proposal (RFP): Companies often issue RFPs in order for potential suppliers to bid on a product or service.

Return on investment (ROI): ROI can be calculated as a percent by taking the net value of monetary benefits divided by the known related costs and multiplying that amount by 100.

Reusable learning object (RLO): A self-contained set of instructional content such as text, assessments and media that supports a learning objective.

Revoked access: Restricting a user from accessing part of the software or website, or the entire product.

Rich Internet application (RIA): An RIA is a Web app with many of the same characteristics as desktop applications. Users generally need to download and install a specific framework in order for an RIA to function properly.

Robo-dial: An automated phone system.

Sandbox: A secure computer area often used to execute untested or unverified computer code.

Scope creep: In project management speak, scope creep is the state of uncontrolled growth in the overall goals or features in a project. This unplanned work costs money, time and often causes a strain on quality as well.

Server-side: Operations performed by the server instead of the client in computer networking.

Services-oriented architecture: A information systems architecture that supports separation of data from business logic and presentation. This allows developers to create "services", or data interfaces that allows data to be sent to an endpoint in a flexbile format that can be consumed or used in a variety of ways.

Shareable Content Object Reference Model (SCORM): A tool used in online training used for packaging content and exchanging data at runtime in order to provide interoperability of content. SCORM "defines a specific way of constructing Learning Management Systems and training content" (*One Minute Overview*).

Short message service (SMS): The text communication service component of phone, Web or mobile communication systems, using standardized communications protocols that allow the exchange of short text messages between fixed-line or mobile phone devices.

Sideloading: The process of transferring data between two local devices. For example, a smartphone could sideload a document from a computer using a USB cable or Bluetooth.

Simulator: A software version of a hardware device used for development and testing.

Skeuomorph: A skeuomorph is a derivative object that retains ornamental design cues to a structure that was necessary in the original. Skeuomorphs may be deliberately employed to make the new look comfortably old and familiar, such as copper cladding on zinc pennies or computer printed postage with circular town name and cancellation lines.

Software as a service (SaaS): Both the software and its data are hosted on a server, allowing users to pull information directly from them. This software is available in a subscription model, rather than through a traditional purchase.

Software development kit (SDK): A set of development tools that allows for the creation of applications for a certain software package, software framework, hardware platform, computer system, video game console, operating system or similar platform. Common tools include debugging aids and other utilities often presented in an integrated development environment (IDE). SDKs also frequently include sample code and supporting technical notes or other supporting documentation to help clarify points from the primary reference material.

Subject matter expert (SME): The professional in the organization who knows an expanse of knowledge on a subject and is then used to help create instructional materials based on their experience and expertise.

Sound synthesis: The digital creation of audio waveforms.

Supply chain management (SCM): The design and execution of the supply chain for a company. This is ultimately how the finished product is brought to market.

Telematics: Using computers together with telecommunications systems.

Ticketing application: An issue tracking system manages issues within an organization.

Unique device identifier (UDID): A sequence of 40 characters specific to an iOS device.

Universal Product Code (UPC): The barcode on a product used for sales and inventory tracking.

Use case: The interactions, processes and steps needed to perform a specific task. A core element of user experience focused software design.

User experience (UX): The creation of the architecture and interaction models that affect user experience of a device or system. The purpose of UX is to positively impact the overall experience a person has with a particular interactive system, and its provider. User experience design most frequently defines a sequence of interactions between a user (individual person) and a system, virtual or physical, designed to meet or support user needs and goals, primarily, while also satisfying systems requirements and organizational objectives.

User interface (UI): Also known as a graphical user interface (GUI). This is where people interact with machines. A good UI lets people effectively operate and control the machine, and the machine will provide feedback to people performing the actions. A UI is the true look and feel of the experience of using a mobile device.

Version history: The process of assigning different version names to unique software releases.

Virtual private network (VPN): This secure network lets users use the Internet, for example, in order to access a central network.

Wayfinding: Orienting people in physical space.

Web-based training (WBT): Another commonly used word for eLearning.

Web services: A method of machine-to-machine interaction over a network.

Wireframe: A diagram format used to aid in the design and creation of software and Web products. This blueprint-like document focuses on the content elements and functional pieces of the product and shies away from using color or specific imagery. Wireframes offer a great deal of detail about what a page or application can and cannot do, without requiring a significant amount of time to be spent on graphic design.

WikiSpaces: An online wiki software provider.

Xcode: The Mac OS X IDE used to develop applications for both the desktop operating system (currently OS X) iOS, which is used on iPhones, iPads and iPod Touch devices.

XLS: The file extension for Excel spreadsheet. Also can be saved in a .xlsx format.

APPENDIX B

REFERENCES

10,000,000 strong. (2011). Retrieved April 18, 2012, from https://foursquare.com/infographics/10million

2012 mobile future in focus: Key insights from 2011 and what they mean for the coming year. (2012, February). Retrieved from comScore website: http://www.comscore.com/Press_Events/Presentations_Whitepapers/2012/2012_Mobile_Future_in_Focus

About QRcode.com. (n.d.). Retrieved April 27, 2012, from http://www.denso-wave.com/qrcode/index-e.html

Adkins, S. S. (2011, May). *The US market for mobile learning products and services: 2010-2015 forecast and analysis.* Retrieved from http://www.ambientinsight.com/Reports/MobileLearning.aspx#section1

Allen, M. (2009). *Michael Allen's e-learning annual 2009.* Retrieved from http://my.safaribooksonline.com/book/hr-organizational-management/9780470371459

Ambient light sensors. (n.d.). [Brochure]. Retrieved from http://www.vishay.com/docs/49670/pl0366.pdf

Apple reports second quarter results [Press release]. (2012, April 24). Retrieved April 27, 2012, from http://www.apple.com/pr/library/2012/04/24Apple-Reports-Second-Quarter-Results.html

Atwood, J. (2006, June 28). The mysterious cone of uncertainty [Web log post]. Retrieved from http://www.codinghorror.com/blog/2006/06/the-mysterious-cone-of-uncertainty.html

Barncard, C. (2011, October 11). *Bird song app identifies feathered friends by tweets.* Retrieved April 27, 2012, from University of Wisconsin-Madison website: http://www.news.wisc.edu/19882

Canny, J. (1986, November). A computational approach to edge detection. *IEEE Transactions on Pattern Analysis and Machine Intelligence, 8*(6), 679-698. doi:10.1109/TPAMI.1986.4767851

Chen, B. X. (2009, August 25). If you're not seeing data, you're not seeing [Web log post]. Retrieved from http://www.wired. com/gadgetlab/2009/08/augmented-reality/

Clark, J. (2010). *Tapworthy: Designing great iPhone apps*. Sebastopol, CA: O'Reilly Media.

comScore reports December 2011 U.S. mobile subscriber market share. (2012, February 2). Retrieved April 10, 2012, from http://www.comscore. com/Press_Events/Press_Releases/2012/2/comScore_Reports_ December_2011_U.S._Mobile_Subscriber_Market_Share

comScore reports December 2009 U.S. mobile subscriber market share. (2010, February 8). Retrieved April 10, 2012, from http://www.comscore. com/Press_Events/Press_Releases/2010/2/comScore_Reports_ December_2009_U.S._Mobile_Subscriber_Market_Share

comScore reports December 2010 U.S. mobile subscriber market share. (2011, February 7). Retrieved April 10, 2012, from http://www.comscore. com/Press_Events/Press_Releases/2011/2/comScore_Reports_ December_2010_U.S._Mobile_Subscriber_Market_Share

Cross, J. (2007). *Informal learning: Rediscovering the natural pathways that inspire innovation and performance*. San Francisco, CA: Pfeiffer.

Cummings, M. (2009, May 8). Information architecture [Web log post]. Retrieved from http://www.interaction-design. org/encyclopedia/information_architecture.html

Darwell, B. (2012, April 5). 200M users include location in Facebook posts; Company looks to expand location APIs [Web log post]. Retrieved from http://www.insidefacebook.com/2012/04/05/200m-users-include-loca- tion-in-facebook-posts-company-looks-to-expand-location-apis/

Evans, B. (2011, December 27). Facebook's 300m app users [Web log post]. Retrieved from http://www.ben-evans.com/post/14858334056/faceboo ks-300m-app-users

Falaki, H., Mahajan, R., Kandula, S., Lymberopoulos, D., Govindan, R., & Estrin, D. (2010). *Diversity in smartphone usage*. Retrieved from Department of Computer Science, University of California, Los Angeles website: http://www.cs.ucla.edu/~falaki/

Farago, P. (2011, October 31). iOS & Android apps challenged by traffic acquisition not discovery [Web log post]. Retrieved from http://blog. flurry.com/bid/76874/iOS-Android-Apps-Challenged-by-Traffic-Acqui- sition-Not-Discovery

Fed Ex stolen idea [Video file]. (n.d.). Retrieved from http://www.youtube. com/watch?v=zNCrMEOqHpc

Ferolo, J., Adams, E., Beuhler, C., Childs, G., Darling, A., Findley, M., . . .
Zimmermann, A. (2011). *Mobile use patterns: Advertising, modalities
and calls to action via mobile devices*. Retrieved from: http://www.ferolo.
com/downloads/mobile-research.pdf

Foster, D. (2006, September 25). Using wikis for corporate collaboration [Web log post]. Retrieved from http://software.intel.com/en-
us/blogs/2006/09/25/using-wikis-for-corporate-collaboration/

Geocaching. (n.d.). Retrieved April 18, 2012, from http://en.wikipedia.
org/wiki/Geocaching

Global PND shipments declined to 33 million units in 2011. (2012, January
17). Retrieved April 27, 2012, from http://www.berginsight.com/News.
aspx?s_m=1&m_m=6

Good Technology state of BYOD report. (2011, December). Retrieved from
http://www.good.com/resources/Good_Data_BYOD_2011.pdf

Gottfredson, C., & Mosher, B. (2010). *Innovative performance support: Strategies and practices for learning in the workflow.* McGraw-Hill.

Green, M., & McGill, E. (2011, December). *State of the industry, 2011:
ASTD's annual review of workplace learning and development data*
(L. Miller, G. Saltzmann, A. McDonald, & S. Castellano, Eds.).
Retrieved from ASTD website: http://store.astd.org/Default.
aspx?tabid=167&ProductId=22697

Halvorson, K. (2008, December 16). The discipline of content strategy
[Web log post]. Retrieved from http://www.alistapart.com/articles/thedi
sciplineofcontentstrategy/

Hesseldahl, A. (2011, October 19). Say, when did Apple become an enterprise company? [Web log post]. Retrieved from http://allthingsd.
com/20111019/say-when-did-apple-become-an-enterprise-company/

Human performance improvement program. (n.d.). Retrieved May 1, 2012,
from http://www.astd.org/Education/Human-Performance-Improve-
ment-Programs

Kellogg, D. (2011, June 17). Average U.S. smartphone data usage up by
89% as cost per MB does down 46% [Web log post]. Retrieved from
http://blog.nielsen.com/nielsenwire/online_mobile/average-u-s-smart-
phone-data-usage-up-89-as-cost-per-mb-goes-down-46/

Kony Solutions, Inc.'s second annual mobile marketing and commerce study.
(2011, September). Retrieved from http://www.kony.com/kony-mobile-
marketing-commerce-study-2011

Lasica, J. D. (2010, July 28). The story of Intelpedia: A model corporate wiki [Web log post]. Retrieved from http://www.socialmedia. biz/2010/07/08/the-story-of-intelpedia-a-model-corporate-wiki/

Livingstone, D. W. (1999). *Exploring the icebergs of adult learning: Findings of the first Canadian survey of informal learning practices.* Retrieved from https://tspace.library.utoronto.ca/retrieve/4451/10exploring.pdf

Lykins, L., & Wentworth, D. (2011). *Mobile learning: Learning in the palm of your hand* (L. Miller, A. McDonald, M. Green, E. McGill, & L. Fox, Eds.). Retrieved from ASTD website: http://www.astd. org/Publications/Research-Reports/2011-Mobile-Learning

Manifesto for agile software development. (2001). Retrieved April 19, 2012, from http://agilemanifesto.org/

Masie, E. (2010, February 19). Goodbye, Training Magazine; Social learning survey data [Web log post]. Retrieved from http://trends. masie.com/archives/2010/2/19/607-goodbye-training-magazine-social-learning-survey-data.html

Merrill, M. D., Drake, L., Lacy, M. J., & Pratt, J. (1996). Reclaiming instructional design. *Educational Technology, 36*(5), 5-7. Retrieved from http://mdavidmerrill.com/Papers/papers.htm

Natalie. (2011, February 14). Facebook photo trends [INFOGRAPHIC] [Web log post]. Retrieved from http://blog.pixable.com/2011/02/14/facebook-photo-trends-infographic/

Newark-French, C. (2011, August 31). Mobile app inventory hungry enough to eat Internet display ad spend [Web log post]. Retrieved from http://blog.flurry.com/bid/71285/Mobile-App-Inventory-Hungry-Enough-to-Eat-Internet-Display-Ad-Spend

New book by Bob Mosher about performance support [press release]. (2011, February 1). Retrieved April 27, 2012, from http://www.ontuitive. com/resources/news-and-events/news/new-book-bob-mosher-about-performance-support

O'Leonard, K. (2011, April 20). Corporate spending on social learning [Web log post]. Retrieved from http://blogs.bersin. com/blog/post/2011/04/Corporate-Spending-on-Social-Learning.aspx

Pfeiffer, D. (2011, July 12). Which cross-platform framework is right for me? [Web log post]. Retrieved from http://floatlearning. com/2011/07/which-cross-platform-framework-is-right-for-me/

Phillips, P. P. (2012). *The bottomline on ROI* (2nd ed.). HRDQ.

Rainie, L., Zickuhr, K., Purcell, K., Madden, M., & Brenner, J. (2012, April 5). *The rise of e-reading.* Retrieved from http://libraries.pewinternet. org/2012/04/04/the-rise-of-e-reading/

Raybould, B. (1995). Performance support engineering: An emerging development methodology for enabling organizational learning. *Performance Improvement Quarterly, 8*(1), 7-22.

Schmit, J. (2008, May 16). No left turn: Companies try to save fuel as prices rise. *USA Today.* Retrieved from http://www.usatoday.com/money/industries/energy/2008-04-30-fuel-costs-companies_N.htm

Slocum, M. (2010, July 15). *Mobile accelerometers and gyroscopes explained.* Retrieved April 28, 2012, from http://answers.oreilly.com/topic/1751-mobile-accelerometers-and-gyroscopes-explained/

Smith, A. (2011, September 19). *Americans and text messaging.* Retrieved from http://pewinternet.org/Reports/2011/Cell-Phone-Texting-2011. aspx

Taylor, Craig (2002). E-Learning: the second wave. Learning Circuits, Oct.

Tapscott, D., Ticoll, D., & Lowy, A. (2000). *Digital capital: Harnessing the power of business webs.* Harvard Business School Press.

The one minute SCORM overview for anyone. (n.d.). Retrieved May 1, 2012, from Rustici Software website: http://scorm.com/scorm-explained/one-minute-scorm-overview/

The world in 2011: ICT facts and figures. (2011, October 25). [Brochure]. Retrieved from http://www.itu.int/ITU-D/ict/facts/2011/index.html

United Airlines launches paperless flight deck with iPad [Press release]. (2011, August 23). Retrieved May 3, 2012, from http://ir.unitedcontinentalholdings.com/phoenix.zhtml?c=83680&p=irol-newsArticle&ID=1599253

V431. (2007, October 3). BMW augmented reality [Video file]. Retrieved from http://www.youtube.com/watch?v=P9KPJlA5yds

Willv. (2011, January 25). Anatomy of a QR code [Web log post]. Retrieved from http://www.betterresponseblog.com/index.php/industry-trends/anatomy-of-a-qr-code/

Woodill, G., & Udell, C. (2011, November). *Calculating the ROI of your mobile learning initiative.* Retrieved from http://floatlearning.com/research-papers/

Worldwide smartphone market expected to grow 55% in 2011 and approach shipments of one billion in 2015, according to IDC. (2011, June 9). Retrieved April 20, 2012, from http://www.idc.com/getdoc. jsp?containerId=prUS22871611

APPENDIX C

RECOMMENDED READING

Gawande, A. (2009). *The checklist manifesto: How to get things right*. New York, NY: Metropolitan Books.

Gery, G. J. (1995). *Electronic performance support systems: How and why to remake the workplace through the strategic application of technology*. Tolland, MA: Gery Performance Press.

Hoober, S., & Berkman, E. (2011). *Designing mobile interfaces*. Sebastopol, CA: O'Reilly Media.

Illich, I. (1971). *Deschooling society*. Calder & Boyars.

Illich, I., & Verne, E. (1976). *Imprisoned in the classroom*. Writers and Readers.

McConnell, S. (2006). *Best Practices (Microsoft): Software estimation: Demystifying the black art*. Redmond, WA: Microsoft Press.

Medina, J. (2008). *Brain rules: 12 principles for surviving and thriving at work, home, and school*. Seattle, WA: Pear Press.

Meyer, E. (2006). *CSS: The definitive guide* (3rd ed.). Sebastopol, CA: O'Reilly Media.

Pilgrim, M. (2010). *HTML5: Up and running*. Sebastopol, CA: O'Reilly Media.

Quinn, C. (2011a). *The mobile academy: mLearning for higher education*. San Francisco, CA: Jossey-Bass.

Quinn, C. (2011b). *Designing mLearning: Tapping into the mobile revolution for organizational performance*. San Francisco, CA: Pfeiffer.

Recent recommender systems research. (n.d.). Retrieved April 27, 2012, from http://www.mendeley.com/groups/501661/recent-recommender-systems-research/

Robbins, J. N. (2007). *Learning web design: A beginner's guide to (X)HTML, stylesheets, and Web graphics*. Sebastopol, CA: O'Reilly Media.

Saffer, D. (2009). *Designing gestural interfaces: Touchscreens and interactive devices*. Sebastopol, CA: O'Reilly Media.

Segaran, T. (2007). *Programming collective intelligence: Building smart Web 2.0 applications.* Sebastopol, CA: O'Reilly Media.

Woodill, G. (2010). *The mobile learning edge: Tools and technologies for developing your teams.* New York, NY: McGraw-Hill.

Zeldman, J., & Marcotte, E. (2009). *Designing with Web standards* (3rd ed.). Berkeley, CA: New Riders. (Original work published 2003)

INDEX